Mental Ability and Higher Educational Attainment

*The Carnegie Commission on Higher Education,
1947 Center Street, Berkeley, California 94704,
has sponsored preparation of this report as a
part of a continuing effort to obtain and present
significant information for public discussion.
The views expressed are those of the authors.*

Copyright © 1972 by
Carnegie Commission on Higher Education
1947 Center Street
Berkeley, California 94704
and National Bureau of Economic Research
261 Madison Avenue
New York, New York 10016

All Rights Reserved
Library of Congress Catalog Card Number: 77-171575
ISBN 0-87014-243-7
Printed in the United States of America

Mental Ability and Higher Educational Attainment in the 20th Century

by *Paul Taubman*
Professor of Economics
University of Pennsylvania

and *Terence Wales*
Associate Professor of Economics
University of British Columbia

---

*A Technical Report Prepared for
The Carnegie Commission on Higher Education*

National Bureau of Economic Research
Occasional Paper 118

Carnegie Commission on Higher Education
Sponsored Research Studies

PROFESSIONAL EDUCATION:
SOME NEW DIRECTIONS
Edgar H. Schein

THE NONPROFIT RESEARCH INSTITUTE:
ITS ORIGIN, OPERATION, PROBLEMS,
AND PROSPECTS
Harold Orlans

THE INVISIBLE COLLEGES:
A PROFILE OF SMALL, PRIVATE
COLLEGES WITH LIMITED RESOURCES
Alexander W. Astin and Calvin B. T. Lee

AMERICAN HIGHER EDUCATION:
DIRECTIONS OLD AND NEW
Joseph Ben-David

A DEGREE AND WHAT ELSE?:
CORRELATES AND CONSEQUENCES OF
A COLLEGE EDUCATION
Stephen B. Withey, Jo Anne Coble, Gerald Gurin, John P. Robinson, Burkhard Strumpel, Elizabeth Keogh Taylor, and Arthur C. Wolfe

THE MULTICAMPUS UNIVERSITY:
A STUDY OF ACADEMIC GOVERNANCE
Eugene C. Lee and Frank M. Bowen

INSTITUTIONS IN TRANSITION:
A PROFILE OF CHANGE IN HIGHER
EDUCATION
(INCORPORATING THE 1970
STATISTICAL REPORT)
Harold L. Hodgkinson

EFFICIENCY IN LIBERAL EDUCATION:
A STUDY OF COMPARATIVE INSTRUC-
TIONAL COSTS FOR DIFFERENT WAYS
OF ORGANIZING TEACHING-LEARNING
IN A LIBERAL ARTS COLLEGE
Howard R. Bowen and Gordon K. Douglass

CREDIT FOR COLLEGE:
PUBLIC POLICY FOR STUDENT LOANS
Robert W. Hartman

MODELS AND MAVERICKS:
A PROFILE OF PRIVATE LIBERAL
ARTS COLLEGES
Morris T. Keeton

BETWEEN TWO WORLDS:
A PROFILE OF NEGRO HIGHER
EDUCATION
Frank Bowles and Frank A. DeCosta

BREAKING THE ACCESS BARRIERS:
A PROFILE OF TWO-YEAR COLLEGES
Leland L. Medsker and Dale Tillery

ANY PERSON, ANY STUDY:
AN ESSAY ON HIGHER EDUCATION IN
THE UNITED STATES
Eric Ashby

THE NEW DEPRESSION IN HIGHER
EDUCATION:
A STUDY OF FINANCIAL CONDITIONS
AT 41 COLLEGES AND UNIVERSITIES
Earl F. Cheit

FINANCING MEDICAL EDUCATION:
AN ANALYSIS OF ALTERNATIVE
POLICIES AND MECHANISMS
Rashi Fein and Gerald I. Weber

HIGHER EDUCATION IN NINE
COUNTRIES:
A COMPARATIVE STUDY OF COLLEGES
AND UNIVERSITIES ABROAD
Barbara B. Burn, Philip G. Altbach, Clark Kerr, and James A. Perkins

BRIDGES TO UNDERSTANDING:
INTERNATIONAL PROGRAMS OF AMER-
ICAN COLLEGES AND UNIVERSITIES
Irwin T. Sanders and Jennifer C. Ward

GRADUATE AND PROFESSIONAL
EDUCATION, 1980:
A SURVEY OF INSTITUTIONAL PLANS
Lewis B. Mayhew

THE AMERICAN COLLEGE AND
AMERICAN CULTURE:
SOCIALIZATION AS A FUNCTION OF
HIGHER EDUCATION
Oscar and Mary F. Handlin

RECENT ALUMNI AND HIGHER
EDUCATION:
A SURVEY OF COLLEGE GRADUATES
Joe L. Spaeth and Andrew M. Greeley

CHANGE IN EDUCATIONAL POLICY:
SELF-STUDIES IN SELECTED COLLEGES
AND UNIVERSITIES
Dwight R. Ladd

STATE OFFICIALS AND HIGHER
EDUCATION:
A SURVEY OF THE OPINIONS AND
EXPECTATIONS OF POLICY MAKERS IN
NINE STATES
Heinz Eulau and Harold Quinley

ACADEMIC DEGREE STRUCTURES:
INNOVATIVE APPROACHES
PRINCIPLES OF REFORM IN DEGREE
STRUCTURES IN THE UNITED STATES
Stephen H. Spurr

COLLEGES OF THE FORGOTTEN
AMERICANS:
A PROFILE OF STATE COLLEGES
AND REGIONAL UNIVERSITIES
E. Alden Dunham

FROM BACKWATER TO MAINSTREAM:
A PROFILE OF CATHOLIC HIGHER
EDUCATION
Andrew M. Greeley

THE ECONOMICS OF THE MAJOR
PRIVATE UNIVERSITIES
William G. Bowen
(Out of print, but available from University Microfilms.)

THE FINANCE OF HIGHER EDUCATION
Howard R. Bowen
(Out of print, but available from University Microfilms.)

ALTERNATIVE METHODS OF FEDERAL
FUNDING FOR HIGHER EDUCATION
Ron Wolk

INVENTORY OF CURRENT RESEARCH
ON HIGHER EDUCATION 1968
Dale M. Heckman and Warren Bryan Martin

The following technical reports are available from the Carnegie Commission on Higher Education, 1947 Center Street, Berkeley, California 94704.

SOURCES OF FUNDS TO COLLEGES
AND UNIVERSITIES
June O'Neill

MAY 1970:
THE CAMPUS AFTERMATH OF
CAMBODIA AND KENT STATE
Richard E. Peterson and John A. Bilorusky

TRENDS AND PROJECTIONS OF PHYSI-
CIANS IN THE UNITED STATES 1967-2002
Mark S. Blumberg

RESOURCE USE IN HIGHER EDUCATION:
TRENDS IN OUTPUT AND INPUTS,
1930-1967
June O'Neill

MENTAL ABILITY AND HIGHER
EDUCATIONAL ATTAINMENT
IN THE 20TH CENTURY
Paul Taubman and Terence Wales

The following reprints are available from the Carnegie Commission on Higher Education, 1947 Center Street, Berkeley, California 94704. (First copies of reprints are sent free on request. Enclose 20 cents each for additional copies to defray costs of postage and handling.)

FACULTY UNIONISM: FROM THEORY TO PRACTICE, *by Joseph W. Garbarino, reprinted from* INDUSTRIAL RELATIONS, *vol. 11, no. 1, pp. 1-17, February 1972.*

INTERNATIONAL PROGRAMS OF U.S. COLLEGES AND UNIVERSITIES: PRIORITIES FOR THE SEVENTIES, *by James A. Perkins, Occasional Paper No. 1, July 1971, reprinted by permission of the International Council for Educational Development.*

ACCELERATED PROGRAMS OF MEDICAL EDUCATION, *by Mark S. Blumberg, reprinted from* JOURNAL OF MEDICAL EDUCATION, *vol. 46, no. 8, August 1971.*

SCIENTIFIC MANPOWER FOR 1970-1985, *by Allan M. Cartter, reprinted from* SCIENCE, *vol. 172, no. 3979, pp. 132-140, April 9, 1971.*

A NEW METHOD OF MEASURING STATES' HIGHER EDUCATION BURDEN, *by Neil Timm, reprinted from* THE JOURNAL OF HIGHER EDUCATION, *vol. 42, no. 1, pp. 27-33, January 1971.*

REGENT WATCHING, *by Earl F. Cheit, reprinted from* AGB REPORTS, *vol. 13, no. 6, pp. 4-13, March 1971.* *

COLLEGE GENERATIONS—FROM THE 1930's TO THE 1960's, *by Seymour M. Lipset and Everett C. Ladd, Jr., reprinted from* THE PUBLIC INTEREST, *no. 24, Summer 1971.*

AMERICAN SOCIAL SCIENTISTS AND THE GROWTH OF CAMPUS POLITICAL ACTIVISM IN THE 1960s, *by Everett C. Ladd, Jr., and Seymour M. Lipset, reprinted from* SOCIAL SCIENCES INFORMATION, *vol. 10, no. 2, April 1971.*

THE POLITICS OF AMERICAN POLITICAL SCIENTISTS, *by Everett C. Ladd, Jr., and Seymour M. Lipset, reprinted from* PS, *vol. 4, no. 2, Spring 1971.* *

THE DIVIDED PROFESSORIATE, *by Seymour M. Lipset and Everett C. Ladd, Jr., reprinted from* CHANGE, *vol. 3, no. 3, pp. 54-60, May 1971.*

JEWISH AND GENTILE ACADEMICS IN THE UNITED STATES: ACHIEVEMENTS, CULTURES AND POLITICS, *by Seymour M. Lipset and Everett C. Ladd, Jr., reprinted from* AMERICAN JEWISH YEAR BOOK, *1971.*

THE UNHOLY ALLIANCE AGAINST THE CAMPUS, *by Kenneth Keriston and Michael Lerner, reprinted from* NEW YORK TIMES MAGAZINE, *November 8, 1970.*

PRECARIOUS PROFESSORS: NEW PATTERNS OF REPRESENTATION, *by Joseph W. Garbarino, reprinted from* INDUSTRIAL RELATIONS, *vol. 10, no. 1, February 1971.*

... AND WHAT PROFESSORS THINK: ABOUT STUDENT PROTEST AND MANNERS, MORALS, POLITICS, AND CHAOS ON THE CAMPUS, *by Seymour Martin Lipset and Everett Carll Ladd, Jr., reprinted from* PSYCHOLOGY TODAY, *November 1970.* *

DEMAND AND SUPPLY IN U.S. HIGHER EDUCATION: A PROGRESS REPORT, by Roy Radner and Leonard S. Miller, reprinted from AMERICAN ECONOMIC REVIEW, May 1970.*

RESOURCES FOR HIGHER EDUCATION: AN ECONOMIST'S VIEW, by Theodore W. Schultz, reprinted from JOURNAL OF POLITICAL ECONOMY, vol. 76, no. 3, University of Chicago, May/June 1968.*

INDUSTRIAL RELATIONS AND UNIVERSITY RELATIONS, by Clark Kerr, reprinted from PROCEEDINGS OF THE 21ST ANNUAL WINTER MEETING OF THE INDUSTRIAL RELATIONS RESEARCH ASSOCIATION, pp. 15-25.*

NEW CHALLENGES TO THE COLLEGE AND UNIVERSITY, by Clark Kerr, reprinted from Kermit Gordon (ed.), AGENDA FOR THE NATION, The Brookings Institution, Washington, D.C., 1968.*

PRESIDENTIAL DISCONTENT, by Clark Kerr, reprinted from David C. Nichols (ed.) PERSPECTIVES ON CAMPUS TENSIONS: PAPERS PREPARED FOR THE SPECIAL COMMITTEE ON CAMPUS TENSIONS. American Council on Education, Washington, D.C., September 1970.*

STUDENT PROTEST—AN INSTITUTIONAL AND NATIONAL PROFILE, by Harold Hodgkinson, reprinted from THE RECORD, vol. 71, no. 4, May 1970.*

WHAT'S BUGGING THE STUDENTS?, by Kenneth Keniston, reprinted from EDUCATIONAL RECORD, American Council on Education, Washington, D.C., Spring 1970.*

THE POLITICS OF ACADEMIA, by Seymour Martin Lipset, reprinted from David C. Nichols (ed.), PERSPECTIVES ON CAMPUS TENSIONS: PAPERS PREPARED FOR THE SPECIAL COMMITTEE ON CAMPUS TENSIONS, American Council on Education, Washington, D.C., September 1970.*

*The Commission's stock of this reprint has been exhausted.

RELATION OF THE DIRECTORS TO THE WORK AND PUBLICATIONS OF THE NATIONAL BUREAU OF ECONOMIC RESEARCH

1. The object of the National Bureau of Economic Research is to ascertain and to present to the public important economic facts and their interpretation in a scientific and impartial manner. The Board of Directors is charged with the responsibility of ensuring that the work of the National Bureau is carried on in strict conformity with this object.

2. The President of the National Bureau shall submit to the Board of Directors, or to its Executive Committee, for their formal adoption all specific proposals for research to be instituted.

3. No research report shall be published until the President shall have submitted to each member of the Board the manuscript proposed for publication, and such information as will, in his opinion and in the opinion of the author, serve to determine the suitability of the report for publication in accordance with the principles of the National Bureau. Each manuscript shall contain a summary drawing attention to the nature and treatment of the problem studied, the character of the data and their utilization in the report, and the main conclusions reached.

4. For each manuscript so submitted, a special committee of the Board shall be appointed by majority agreement of the President and Vice Presidents (or by the Executive Committee in case of inability to decide on the part of the President and Vice Presidents), consisting of three directors selected as nearly as may be one from each general division of the Board. The names of the special manuscript committee shall be stated to each director when the manuscript is submitted to him. It shall be the duty of each member of the special manuscript committee to read the manuscript. If each member of the manuscript committee signifies his approval within thirty days of the transmittal of the manuscript, the report may be published. If at the end of that period any member of the manuscript committee withholds his approval, the President shall then notify each member of the Board, requesting approval or disapproval of publication, and thirty days additional shall be granted for this purpose. The manuscript shall then not be published unless at least a majority of the entire Board who shall have voted on the proposal within the time fixed for the receipt of votes shall have approved.

5. No manuscript may be published, though approved by each member of the special manuscript committee, until forty-five days have elapsed from the transmittal of the report in manuscript form. The

interval is allowed for the receipt of any memorandum of dissent or reservation, together with a brief statement of his reasons, that any member may wish to express; and such memorandum of dissent or reservation shall be published with the manuscript if he so desires. Publication does not, however, imply that each member of the Board has read the manuscript, or that either members of the Board in general or the special committee have passed on its validity in every detail.

6. Publications of the National Bureau issued for informational purposes concerning the work of the Bureau and its staff, or issued to inform the public of activities of Bureau staff, and volumes issued as a result of various conferences involving the National Bureau shall contain a specific disclaimer noting that such publication has not passed through the normal review procedures required in this resolution. The Executive Committee of the Board is charged with review of all such publications from time to time to ensure that they do not take on the character of formal research reports of the National Bureau, requiring formal Board approval.

7. Unless otherwise determined by the Board or exempted by the terms of paragraph 6, a copy of this resolution shall be printed in each National Bureau publication.

(Resolution adopted October 25, 1926 and revised February 6, 1933, February 24, 1941, and April 20, 1968)

Foreword

Among the nagging questions about the effectiveness of American higher education are these:

Is the average mental ability level of students being maintained as the system expands?

Do current circumstances affecting accessibility of college and university education to young people still result in any significant loss of talent?

By answering these questions (affirmatively) and by providing empirical evidence to substantiate their findings, the authors of this report of the National Bureau of Economic Research for the Carnegie Commission on Higher Education have rendered a valuable service.

Clark Kerr
Chairman
Carnegie Commission
on Higher Education

March 1972

Foreword

This report is the first in a series of joint publications by the Carnegie Commission on Higher Education and the National Bureau of Economic Research on the subject of returns to higher education. These studies attempt to go beyond measuring only private rewards from higher education by focusing as well on possible social benefits derived from postsecondary schooling.

The present volume, however, differs somewhat in stress from the publications yet to come. This study is, in fact, a by-product of a larger study by Paul Taubman and Terence Wales in which they attempt to measure the effects of ability on earnings and thereby hope to calculate the returns to educational investment.

In this report, Taubman and Wales are concerned with a longstanding debate in educational circles within the United States. Specifically, they examine whether the rapid increase in the number of high school students who have entered colleges and universities in the United States in recent decades has resulted in a deterioration of the academic quality of college students. Although one could wish that more data were available, the authors have used the data developed for their larger study to present what must be considered the best empirical evaluation of this question to date. Taubman and Wales conclude that on the basis of their tests and findings, student quality has not deteriorated in the United States as the student population and percentage of youths matriculating has expanded.

Many aspects and objectives of the recent American experiment with mass higher education may remain in doubt. However, there now seems to be little factual basis for discrediting that experiment on the grounds that in the past it has lowered the ability level of students attending universities and colleges in the United States.

John R. Meyer
President
National Bureau
of Economic Research

March 1972

Contents

Forewords, xi

Preface and Acknowledgements, xv

1 *Introduction and Summary of Findings, 1*

2 *Possible Measures of Mental Ability and Educational Attainment, 7*

3 *Conceptual and Statistical Problems, 11*
  Causality vs. description ▪ *Effect of education on mental ability*

4 *Conclusions, 17*

  Appendix A: Data and Results from the Various Studies Used in this Report, 25

  Appendix B: Other Studies, 41

  Appendix C: Adjustment Procedures for Average-Ability and Loss-of-Talent Calculations, 43

  References, 45

Preface and Acknowledgements

Several years ago we began a study of the rate of return to higher education. In such a study we were faced with the difficult though well-known problem that income differences by educational level in census data arise partly because the more educated are also brighter. There are a number of ways to overcome the "ability" problem. One such method, which we examined early in the study, was based on the proposition that the relationship between mental ability and education may have shifted for people born in different time intervals.

We started with an assumption that around 1920, high school graduates were no different from those who went to college, but that over time those who went to college became progressively more able. Several people objected that they would expect the exact opposite, with an ability differential greatest for the oldest cohort. To resolve this issue, we decided the simplest thing to do would be to read some histories of higher education to find out the facts in the case. Since changes in the education-ability relationship would be important to many questions and disciplines, we expected that the answer would be readily available. To our surprise, we found little written explicitly on the subject. However it soon became apparent that the necessary information to answer the questions was scattered over a wide number of seemingly unrelated studies.

It is perhaps worth noting that the original method we were exploring did not pan out. This monograph, therefore, reports on the attempt of two economists to extract from noneconomic data some historical relationships that are of primary concern to noneconomists and of secondary concern to economists. We have tried to aid noneconomists by foregoing technical jargon and using English, but the attempt has not always been successful.

This study has benefited from many individuals and groups. Included are, of course, the many scholars listed in the text who over the years conducted well-designed studies and published extensive details on their findings. Since many of the sources are rather obscure, the study would never have come to fruition without the extensive collection in the Penniman Library at the University of Pennsylvania and the Interlibrary lending service.

We wish to thank Dael Wolfle and the late Alfred Conrad, Robert Michael and Finis Welch of the NBER staff reading committee, and Margaret Gordon of the Carnegie Commission for helpful comments. Thanks are also due to the NBER Director's Reading Committee of Erwin Canham, Lazare Teper, and Lloyd Reynolds, as well as to Boris Shiskin and Emilio Collado, whose comments helped to improve the substance and style of the manuscript. We wish to thank Marc Freiman, Peter Gottschalk, and Janet Young for their research assistance, Gnomi Schrift Gouldin and Sidney Hollister, who edited the paper, and H. Irving Forman, who drew the charts. This study was aided by funds from the Carnegie Commission on Higher Education and by general funds of the National Bureau.

Paul Taubman
Terence Wales

1. Introduction and Summary of Findings

Many important changes have occurred in higher education in the United States since 1900. At the turn of the century very few people finished high school, but most of those who did, attended college. For example, only about 7 percent of the population born around 1880, but 70 percent of all high school graduates, entered college. After World War I there was a big increase in the number of students attending high school but a sharp decrease in the fraction of high school graduates attending college.[1] However, after World War II the fraction of high school graduates attending college increased, until by 1970 about 50 percent of the eligible age group and 60 percent of all high school graduates attended college.[2]

The organization of higher education also changed greatly. For example, many four-year colleges changed their status to universities, numerous two-year colleges were founded, and normal schools became teachers colleges, which in turn expanded into standard four-year colleges. As the number of institutions of higher learning has increased, attempts have been made (for example, in California) to integrate community colleges, four-year colleges, and universities into statewide systems of education.[3] Partly in response to the increased demand for higher education at a reasonable cost, state-operated institutions have expanded to become more important in terms of the number of students and the quality of faculties.

The introduction of new courses and a change in emphasis between general and technical education has also shifted the focus of higher education. In part, these changes reflect the formation of new disciplines and the growth in knowledge. However, they also reflect shifts in

---

[1] In part this represented a shift in educational policy toward supplying more education at all levels (Finch, 1946; Folger & Nam, 1967).

[2] These estimates are derived from the methods given in Appendix B. See also Folger and Nam (1967).

[3] See Jencks and Riesman (1968).

the composition of the student population. In 1900, a large fraction of college graduates became medical doctors, lawyers, theologians, or engineers. Since 1900, there has been a marked shift in careers toward business and other professions.[4]

There were several basic causes for these changes. First, there was the need for the educational system to adapt to new conditions in society. These new conditions included the increased demand of the wealthy for education as a consumption or status good; a shift in the occupational mix towards scientific skills; and the belief that education was required to obtain a good job. Second, there was the desire to make as much high-quality education as possible available to all those who could benefit from it.

Change comes no more easily to the academic world than elsewhere. Any alteration in graduation requirements or course offerings raises substantial opposition and debate. Expansion in the size of the university has caused controversy paralleling that of the expansion of high school education.[5] Much of the debate has concerned the need for quality in education and the question of who would or should benefit from higher education.[6]

One particular argument against the expansion of higher and secondary school education has perhaps been raised more than any other. The basis of the argument is that the courses given at most higher-level institutions of learning are oriented towards training people to use mental facilities and certain learning tools to solve various abstract and practical problems. But to be able to acquire the tools and to learn how to solve problems, a person must have a certain threshold level of mental ability or IQ.[7] Therefore, if many students below this threshold level were admitted to institutions of higher learning, the resources they used would be wasted. In addition, the admission of unqualified students in large numbers might interfere with the instruction of those who would benefit from the education.[8]

An argument in favor of expansion points to the "loss in talent" that occurs when many students above the required threshold level cannot

---

[4] See Wolfle (1954).

[5] See, for example, the statement by the president of Harvard in Finch (1946).

[6] It is generally assumed that benefits from education can be measured by the additional future income attributable to education, by the consumption value, and by any external factors such as the value to society of a better functioning democracy.

[7] It is sometimes maintained that the threshold level is at least one-half a standard deviation above the population mean.

[8] This could occur with a class of a very wide range of abilities, if teachers pitched their instructional level too low.

enter college and therefore never have the chance to develop their talents. Some proponents of expansion indicate that excessive heterogeneity in ability levels could be avoided if expansion took the form of added variety in the types of educational institutions.

These viewpoints involve contradictory assertions that can only be resolved by reference to empirical evidence. For higher education in the United States, the facts under dispute are: (1) Did the expansion in college enrollment since 1900 lead to a decline in the average mental ability of college students? (2) Did the expansion lead to a reduction in the loss of talent? (3) At what minimum level of mental ability do individuals (or perhaps society) cease to receive any benefits from education? While these questions are important, very little research has been undertaken to answer them.[9]

Our main interest in this paper is to examine the first two questions by determining the relationship, in various samples spanning the twentieth century, between the percent of high school graduates who enter college and their mental ability at the time of college entrance.[10] The samples used, which are often referred to by name, are drawn from the Project Talent Study and the studies done by Barker, Berdie, Berdie and Hood, Benson, Little, O'Brien, Phearman, Proctor, Wolfle and Smith, and Yerkes. Each of these studies present information on the number of high school graduates entering college by IQ or aptitude test score. To make the tests comparable, we converted the scores to a percentile basis.

The information obtained in answering these two questions can also be used in analyzing other important economic problems. For example, for many purposes in economics it is important to know if the average ability level of persons with various amounts of education has remained constant over age groups. Thus, we may wish to determine how income varies over time for people with a given amount of education. If the average ability level of those with a given amount of education has remained constant over time, we can answer this question by studying income differences for various age groups with a given educational level, as available, say, in the 1960 census. But if the average ability level within an education level is not constant over age groups, the income differences in the census occur because of both age and ability differences.

In addition, the coefficient of education in an equation relating education to mental ability plays an important role in determining the

[9] Partial exceptions are Berdie, et al. (1962) and Darley (1962).

[10] In a recently completed study addressed to the third question, we found that rates of return to higher education do not vary with ability for those in the top half of the ability distribution, except perhaps for people with graduate education and very high ability. See Taubman and Wales (1972).

economic returns to education. It can be shown that when returns to education are estimated using data that do not include a mental-ability variable (such as the census data), the estimated effect of education on income will be biased upward if ability and education are positively related.[11] Further, if this relationship has changed over time, then the bias will change accordingly.

Subject to some qualifications, as given below, our major conclusions are as follows:

1   As shown in Figure 1 the average ability level of high school graduates who entered college ($\bar{A}_c$) ranges from the 53rd to the 63rd percentile (measured upward from zero) for the period 1925 to 1961. Although in the 1930s there was a reduction in the percentage of students entering college, Figure 1 indicates that there was an increase in the average quality of college students compared with the 1920s. On the other hand, the postwar boom in higher education resulted in still higher quality college students than in the 1930s and substantially higher quality students than in the 1920s. The average quality level has increased because initially only about 60 percent of the most able students went to college, while, as shown below, the growth in the fraction entering college is concentrated in the high-ability groups. There is also evidence in Darley (1962) that existing schools have increased the quality of their students while new colleges and community colleges have been started to meet the needs of the less able. Thus the more able students may be receiving a better education now.

2   There has been a significant reduction in the loss of talent since 1920. The loss of talent can be measured by the fraction of high school graduates who enter college at various ability levels. The selected values of ability, measured as percentiles (ranging upward from zero), are 25, 50, 75, and 90. At the 90th and 75th percentiles there has been a substantial increase over time in the percent entering college. At the

---

[11] If the true equation is
(1) $Y = \alpha A + \beta S + u$
where Y is income, A is innate ability, S is educational attainment as measured by highest grade completed, u is a random error term that is independent of A and S, and α and β are parameters to be estimated, then the estimation (by least squares) of the equation $Y = cS$, will yield a coefficient c, with expected value given by:
(2) $E(c) = \beta + k\alpha$
where k is the coefficient from the (least squares) regression,
(3) $A = kS$
Thus, as long as ability is positively related to income ($\alpha > 0$), and as long as educational attainment and ability are positively related (k > 0), then the estimate of c in (2) exceeds β, which, from equation (1), represents the true impact of variations in S on Y.

On the other hand, if we have estimates of the ability-education relationship for various time periods, and if this relationship has changed for various cohorts, it is possible to obtain separate estimates of the effects of education and ability on income in a single cross-section that includes the various cohorts.

Thus, equation (2) expresses the estimated education coefficient in terms of income differential due to education, B, the income differential due to ability, α, and the increase in ability associated with educational changes, k. Since we can obtain an estimate of k, equation (2) has only two unknowns. If another estimate of equation (2) can be obtained in a cohort with a different k, then in principle the two equations can be solved for estimates of both α and B.

FIGURE 1 Average ability levels over time, adjusted

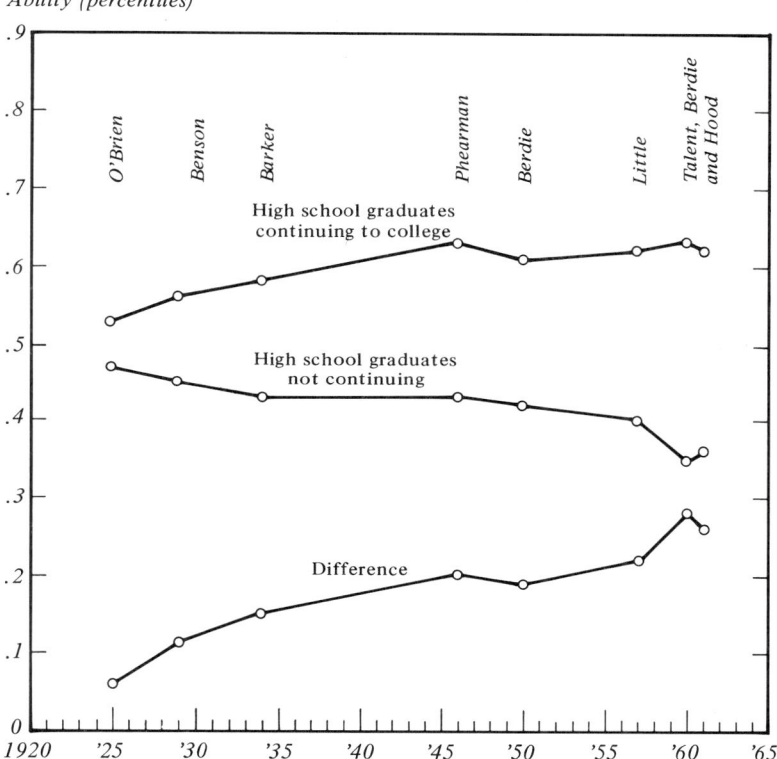

50th percentile the 1960 values are slightly higher than those for the 1920s and the values during the 1930s and 1940s are substantially lower. At the 25th percentile the fraction of high school graduates entering college appears to have fallen during the 1930s and 1940s, but by the 1960s was back to the 1920 level. On the basis of this evidence, we conclude that the substantial increase in the fraction of high school graduates entering college since the 1920s occurred primarily at the 75th and 90th ability percentiles.[12]

It should be realized that these results are subject to a number of qualifications, of which the following are among the most important. Many of our samples are statewide rather than nationwide, and some of the states may be atypical. This difficulty is discussed in more detail on

---

[12] The data (for males) prior to World War I, however, yield a picture similar to that of the 1950s and 1960s. Thus, the big loss of talent at that time occurred prior to high school graduation.

page 43. In addition, the samples use different ability tests that had to be converted to a common basis. Our results, which are based on IQ and aptitude tests, only reflect the mental abilities measured by these tests and not all types of mental ability. Finally, we are assuming that the average ability level of high school seniors in the population has remained constant over time. Although there is some evidence in Berdie, et al. (1962) that this is true, it has not been completely verified.

We turn now to a consideration of the measures of mental ability and education that we used in the analysis. This is followed by a discussion of the major conceptual and statistical problems inherent in the study, our conclusions, and then a detailed presentation of our estimate of the ability-education relationship for each sample.

2. Measures of Mental Ability and Educational Attainment

To measure mental ability it is necessary to know what is being measured and to define a set of units to differentiate between people. Following the approach of psychologists, we conceive of mental ability in terms of the capacity to retain ideas and comprehend and solve abstract problems. While there is no perfect empirical counterpart to this theoretical definition, there are several measures on which differential performance is partly determined by the theoretical construct. The more that differences on the measure are determined by mental ability, the more appropriate is the measure as a proxy.

The two most obvious measures, which should be related to mental ability, are rank in high school class and scores on a standardized set of tests. Although both measures are related to mental ability, one may be a better proxy than the other.

Standardized tests can be divided into IQ and aptitude (achievement) tests. In principle, aptitude tests measure the amount of knowledge or skill acquired (primarily in school) in particular subjects. IQ tests are thought of as measuring general inborn ability, which does not depend upon previous schooling (or the factors noted above). However, a substantial body of evidence suggests that most IQ tests depend, among other things, on years of schooling, quality of schooling, and cultural background.[1] Thus, the difference between IQ and aptitude tests is more a matter of degree than of kind, and we will intermix information from both types of tests as long as the data can be converted to a common scale.

Consider also the differences between test scores and rank in class. One major difficulty of rank-in-class data is that they are computed on the basis of students in a given grade in a single high school, when in fact different schools in the same city often have different quality students, and differences in quality generally exist also between urban and rural schools. Therefore, unless information on the quality of the

---

[1] See for example Learned and Wood (1938).

students is available, it may be misleading to equate the ability of individuals who have the same rank in different schools. On the other hand, the same test may be used in all schools in a system, or, at a minimum, test scores can be standardized over a population. In either case students from various schools can be compared.

Another reason why rank in class can be a very poor proxy of mental ability is that rank may be determined much more by such things as docility in class, memorization, and grades in nonacademic courses. These factors may explain the well-known phenomenon that a disproportionately large percentage of girls are in the higher ranks in class in high school.

An individual's rank in class may, on the other hand, be more dependent on such things as drive and motivation, and these characteristics may be crucial for future academic and career success.[2] Thus some studies, such as Berdie and Hood (1963), have found rank in class slightly more important than IQ or aptitude tests in determining which students enter college. However, contrary evidence exists in Folger and Nam (1967).

Although most studies find that knowledge of both IQ and rank in class significantly improves the prediction of college attendance, we rely on test scores because of the problem of standardization. In order to facilitate a comparison of results from different samples, we converted the ability measures to the same units for all samples. This not only enables us to compare results, but also to combine small samples for estimation purposes, as discussed in detail below. The standardization method that we used was to convert the IQ measure for each sample into percentile terms, with the "norm" being the population of high school graduates. Since most of the samples involve statewide tests of graduating seniors (e.g., Minnesota, Kansas, Iowa), standardization simply consists of transforming the raw IQ measure into within-sample percentile terms. This treatment assumes that the distribution by ability of high school graduates is the same in all states. However, even if the

---

[2] Of course, genetic influences, pre- and postnatal diet, home and school atmosphere, personal motivation, and drive can all affect an individual's intellectual performance as measured by IQ tests or rank in class. To the extent that all the factors that affect class rank or IQ scores are also relevant in determining income, or in determining which are the talented students currently available for college training, then our mental ability index is appropriate in measuring the return to education. Our analysis, of course, is not suitable for determining such magnitudes as the loss of talent that would not have occurred if all children and expectant mothers had had adequate diets.

sample distribution for a state differs from the national norm, the effect will probably be small provided ability is used as the dependent variable.[3]

The main advantage of this conversion method is that it avoids the problem of using conversion tables to compare various raw IQ scores. Such tables contain only the major IQ measures and in many cases appear to be based on small samples. Another advantage of our method is that it permits use of results provided by other investigators in which data are presented only in percentile form. For samples that clearly are not representative of the high school graduate population, we converted the data in a more complicated way.

We assume that the different tests and testing procedures yield data that are comparable. This requires that the rankings of individuals be the same if given the same test at different times or different tests at the same time. Various studies have indicated high reliability (of most tests) for individuals. Even greater reliability should be expected when broad groupings are used; hence, there should be little difficulty in combining the samples. In order to compare and combine samples from different time periods, we make the additional assumption that the average ability level of high school graduates has remained approximately constant over time. Support for this hypothesis is contained in Berdie, et al. (1962), which traces the average ability level of high school graduates in Minnesota from 1928 to 1960, and in which there appears to be no trend in the average ability level as measured by the ACE examination. Further supporting evidence is available in Finch (1946).

We are primarily interested in analyzing post-high school educational attainment. For this purpose it is useful to distinguish two stages in the educational process: entrance into college and length of stay in college. Our analysis is concerned with the former aspect, since the necessary data are more readily available. The basic education measure that we use in analyzing the relation between college entrance and ability is the percentage of high school graduates who enter college.

In this study we do not analyze vocational education because there are virtually no data of the form we need. This suggests that the results of our analysis require careful interpretation. For example, in discussing the loss of talent that results when high-ability students do not attend college, it would be important to know how many of these attended vocational school and if the rate of return to such education was high.

---

[3] This follows because according to the standard results in errors-in-variable problems, if there is an additive measurement error in the dependent variable that is not correlated with the independent variable, we will obtain an unbiased estimate of the slope coefficient. Because of the conversion method used, there is no clear reason for not expecting the measurement errors to meet the above conditions.

Such considerations are particularly relevant in view of the long time period under study and the accompanying changes in emphasis on vocational training. In the 1930s, for example, there was a strong emphasis on this type of education (Anderson and Berning, 1950), although we suspect that in more recent years many equivalent programs have been given by colleges, junior colleges, and community colleges.

3. Conceptual and Statistical Problems

CAUSALITY VS. DESCRIPTION

A question that is of some importance in statistical considerations is the interpretation of the education-ability relationship. That is, does ability "cause" the educational attainment—or vice versa—or does the relationship arise for other reasons.

Let us assume that students and their families have a demand function for educational attainment—for both the consumption and investment aspects. Regardless of whether students want either or both of these aspects, plausible arguments can be made that the demand depends upon the student's ability. Indeed, whether one uses students' educational plans or their actual realization of these plans, a substantial body of evidence exists suggesting that the demand for education is a function of ability.[1] This demand will also depend on such other factors as the family's income level, job and scholarship opportunities, tuition, etc.[2]

On the other hand, educational authorities try to weed out people with low ability levels. What is considered too low may depend upon the physical and budget capacity of the institutions or governments involved. In any event, evidence exists that willingness to promote students to higher grades, to encourage them to stay in school, or to permit them to go to a higher educational institution has varied over time.[3] Thus any observed relationship between educational attainment and ability is the outcome of the factors that affect supply and

---

[1] The plans may be more relevant because one reason that students do not fulfill their plans is that the educational authorities exclude those with low ability. That is, the realization in part reflects supply conditions.

[2] The family's income level affects the demand relation because of imperfect capital markets, differences in tastes for present versus future consumption, and the luxury nature of the consumption of education.

[3] See, for example, Folger and Nam (1967) on the trends in the number of students who were not in the normal school grade of their age group. Consider, also, state and federal provision of support for college facilities.

demand. Shifts in these factors can alter the observed relationship without implying any causation; therefore, we conclude that the data on education and ability should not be interpreted in a causal sense. We will generally use the term "descriptive" to characterize this relationship.

The fact that we interpret the education-ability relation as descriptive provides no guidance for deciding which variable to use as the dependent one in regressions. However, there are two major reasons for using ability as the dependent variable.[4] First, the education-ability relation enables us to correct the bias (of the education coefficient) arising from the omission of ability in income equations. For this purpose we require the education-ability equation to be formulated with education as the independent variable.[5] Second, errors in measuring ability will not bias the coefficient in the regression if ability is used as the dependent variable. There will be a bias if ability is used as the independent variable. On the other hand, there is a rationale for using education as the dependent variable when dealing with certain nonlinear functional relations. That is, one way to test for nonlinearities is to include the independent variable in squared form. This can be accomplished only if ability is the independent variable.[6]

In general, there appear to be no sound reasons for preferring a particular functional form to relate education to ability.[7] For simplicity, we used the linear form. We have, however, tested for nonlinearities by regressing education on ability and ability squared. Where the nonlinearities are significant we indicated the extent to which our conclusions are affected. We also experimented with the logarithmic form but have not presented the results, since this form does not fit well in the tails of the distrubutions, and the estimated coefficients appear to be very sensitive to the scaling of the ability variable—for example, using the midpoints or endpoints of the decile ranks.

---

[4] In addition, for samples in which individuals have different amounts of education when tested, it may be possible to correct the bias when ability is the dependent variable.

[5] This is necessary because, as shown in footnote 11, Chapter 1, in equation (2) the estimate of k is obtained from estimating (by least squares) an equation in which education is the independent variable.

[6] The education variable cannot be included in both unsquared and squared forms as the independent variable because it is obtained by aggregating a zero-one variable, which when squared is still a zero-one dummy variable.

[7] However, for purposes of analyzing the relationship between income, education, and ability, it is necessary that the functional form for the side relation correspond to that of the basic relation. If a dummy variable for college entrance is used in the income analysis, then our linear equation is appropriate. If different dummies are used to represent various educational levels, then our linear equation provides the first step in determining the bias.

There is one minor statistical point that can be dispensed with now. We have been talking interchangeably of the education variable as representing a situation in which an individual does or does not enter college and as representing the fraction of high school graduates entering college. These two concepts can be reconciled as follows. We define a variable D_i as 1 if the ith person enters college and as zero otherwise. Our linear equation for the ith individual is therefore $A_i = h + kD_i$, where A_i is again the ability of the individual. Suppose that we now order the data by ability class and average the observations in each ability group. The education variable then becomes the percentage of people in each ability class who enter college (E_{12}) and the ability variable becomes the average ability level in the class (A).[8]

The linear equation that we estimate for the different samples is therefore $A = h + kE_{12}$. It may be useful at this point to interpret the coefficients h and k. The coefficient h indicates the level of ability at which the fraction of high school graduates entering college is zero. Since in nearly all our samples some students enter college at all ability levels, our estimates of h are generally negative. An alternative interpretation of h may be obtained by solving this equation for E_{12} to give: $E_{12} = -\frac{h}{k} + \frac{1}{k} A$. Provided that h is negative, some students will continue to college even at the lowest ability levels. From this equation, $1/k$ can be interpreted as the increase in the fraction of students entering college for each unit increase in A.

EFFECT OF EDUCATION ON MENTAL ABILITY

Our main interest is in determining the relationship between the percentage of high school graduates entering college and their mental ability at the time of college entrance. The ability measures that we use are various IQ and achievement test scores. These are determined in part by the amount of schooling the individual received prior to taking the tests.

The pioneering study of Learned and Wood (1938) clearly demonstrates the extent to which even IQ measures are affected by years of schooling. In this study nearly 28,000 high school seniors were given a twelve-hour examination in 1928. One part of the examination was the Otis IQ test. Those students who went on to college were retested in eight-hour examinations in 1930 and 1932. Moreover, exactly the same Otis test was given on the last two occasions. Comparing test scores for

---

[8] Formally, this can be accomplished by multiplying by a grouping matrix G whose elements in the ith row (which corresponds to the ith ability group) are zero for all observations not in that ability group and $1/n_i$ for the n_i observations in the group. This gives: $GA_i = hG + kGD_i$. In the ith ability group $GD = n^*_i/n_i$ where n^*_i is the number of people who enter college in that group. Since in the ith group D has n^*_i entries of one and $n_i - n^*_i$ values of zero, its average is n^*_i/n, which is equal to the percentage of people in that ability class who entered college. We denote this percentage as E_{12}.

those in the sample in 1928 and 1930 and those in the sample in 1930 and 1932, it was found that the average score on this test rose 7-1/2 percent from 1928 to 1930 and 5 percent from 1930 to 1932. In other words, the Otis (and presumably all other IQ tests) appear to measure educational attainment as well as mental ability.

Consequently, data from samples in which individuals are subjected to tests after having completed their formal education must be treated differently from those in which all individuals are tested as high school seniors. From a statistical viewpoint, the former problem may be analyzed as an error-in-variables.[9] In nontechnical terms, the problem may be described as follows. People with more education will score higher on tests because of this additional education. Thus it is difficult to distinguish between the effect of education on test scores and the relationship between the mental ability of students at, say, the end of high school and after additional educational attainment. In this case our regression analysis yields biased estimates of the parameters of the

---

[9] We wish to estimate the (descriptive) relationship between educational attainment, S, and mental ability, A. Let the true relationship be expressed as:

(1) $S = \gamma A + u$

Suppose, however, that instead of observing A, we measure IQ where

$IQ = A + z$ and where $E(u,z) = E(A,z) = 0$ but $E(S,z) > 0$

If we use ordinary least squares to estimate the equation $S = gIQ + v$, then:

(2) $\text{plim}(\hat{g}) = \text{plim} \dfrac{\Sigma(S,z) + \gamma \Sigma A^2}{\Sigma(A^2 + z^2)}$

Hence $\hat{g}$ from (2) will, in the limit, exceed γ provided that:

(3) $\dfrac{\Sigma(S,z)}{\Sigma z^2} > \gamma$

But the left-hand side of (3) can be interpreted as the least squares estimate of λ in the equation $S = \lambda z + v$. Thus our estimate of $\hat{g}$ exceeds or falls short of γ, as λ exceeds or falls short of γ, and not even the direction of the (asymptotic) bias is determinable without further information. However, studies such as Learned and Wood contain information on the change in z due to a change in education, and hence we can estimate λ using first differences. This permits us to determine the sign but not the extent of the statistical bias, which in general requires knowledge about $\Sigma A^2 / \Sigma(A^2 + z^2)$.

This ambiguity in the sign of the bias is removed if we postulate the relationship as:

(4) $A = \delta S + w$

Once again we measure A as IQ and regress $IQ = dS$, which yields:

(5) $\text{plim}(\hat{d}) = \delta + \text{plim} \dfrac{\Sigma(S,z)}{\Sigma S^2} > \delta$

Thus with S as the independent variable, our estimate of δ will be biased upward and $\hat{d}$ can be used as an upper limit of δ. Of course it will only be possible to estimate the extent of bias if $\Sigma(S,z) / \Sigma S^2$ is known. But this term is the least squares estimate of ψ in $z = \psi S + v$, and as such measures the contribution of schooling to knowledge or scores on tests. It may be possible to estimate this relationship from data in Learned and Wood.

equation relating ability and education. However, as shown in footnote 23, when education is the independent variable, it may be possible to correct the estimate on the basis of a regression of IQ on additional education.

On the other hand, the relation between ability and education is not obscured if it is estimated from a sample in which IQ's are measured for individuals with the *same* amounts of education at the time of the test.[10] This condition is satisfied by a follow-up survey. By a follow-up survey we mean one in which individuals with the same amount of schooling are tested at a point in time, then their further educational attainment is determined by a future survey. Since all the students will have had the same amount of schooling when they are tested, there can be no differences in the IQ scores that are due to differences in years of schooling.

---

[10]That is, in terms of the errors in variables analysis, the bias arises because z varies between individuals. If z is constant for all individuals then $(z - \bar{z})$ will be equal to zero for each person and all sums involving z's will also be zero.

4 Conclusions

As indicated earlier in this paper, we are interested primarily in answering two questions: Did the expansion in college enrollment since 1900 lead to a decline in the average mental ability of college students? Did it lead to a reduction in the loss of talent? A summary of our results follows.

For the first question, we consider the changes over time in the average ability of students who enter college ($\bar{A}_c$) and in the average ability of those high school graduates who do not enter college ($\bar{A}_{nc}$).[1] We have calculated $\bar{A}_c$ and $\bar{A}_{nc}$ for most of the samples described below.[2] These results for males and females combined are presented in Table 1 in both adjusted and unadjusted form, but only the adjusted values are plotted in Figure 1. The adjustments are made to take into account the difference between the percent of students entering college in each sample and in the country as a whole. A detailed description of this adjustment method is presented in appendix C. In the following discussion we use the adjusted estimates. The $\bar{A}_c$ data suggest a mean IQ of about the 53-63rd percentile for those who enter college. The highest $\bar{A}_c$ is .63 in the Phearman and Talent studies, the lowest is .53 in the O'Brien study.

The general pattern of $\bar{A}_c$ is as follows:[3] During the 1920's $\bar{A}_c$ was at its lowest value—approximately 55 percent. During the 1930's it rose to about 58 percent, and reached a peak of 63 percent in 1946. It

---

[1] We define $\bar{A}_c = \Sigma A_i N_i / \Sigma N_i$ and $\bar{A}_{nc} = \Sigma A_i (1-N_i)/(1-N_i)$. N_i is the fraction of high school graduates in the ith class who entered college times the *population* of high school graduates in the ith class.

[2] For this question the Proctor study is omitted because of its small size, the Yerkes study is omitted because the results are sensitive to the bias correction procedures, and the Wolfle and Smith data are omitted because of the rate of response problem noted below.

[3] One qualification of these results is, as discussed below, that they are drawn from studies involving different states. To the extent that there are differences between states in the college-going behavior of the students, the results may be misleading, although our adjustment method attempts to take this into account.

TABLE 1 Average mental-ability level of high school graduates who entered, and did not enter, college, in various samples

Sample	Date	$\bar{A}_c$	$\bar{A}_{nc}$	$\bar{A}_c - \bar{A}_{nc}$
O'Brien	1925	.54	.47	.07
		.53	.47	.06
Benson	1929	.57	.46	.11
		.56	.45	.11
Barker	1934	.64	.44	.20
		.58	.43	.15
Phearman	1946	.68	.44	.24
		.63	.43	.20
Berdie	1950	.62	.42	.20
		.61	.42	.19
Little	1957	.68	.43	.25
		.62	.40	.22
Talent	1960	.65	.37	.28
		.63	.35	.28
Berdie and Hood	1961	.65	.39	.26
		.62	.36	.26

Note: The first line for each entry is the value calculated from the sample; the second line is this value adjusted to the United States population as a whole. A detailed discussion of the adjustment method appears in appendix C.

remained at approximately this level through 1961, although there may have been a slight dip in the early 1950s. (The dip is more pronounced in the unadjusted data.) While $\bar{A}_c$ was changing, there were also shifts in the fraction of high school graduates entering college. In particular, during the 1930s a smaller fraction of high school graduates attended college than in the 1920s, while during the 1950s and 1960s a larger fraction of graduates entered college than in either of these earlier periods. Thus the reduction in college enrollment in the 1930s resulted in an increase in the average quality of college students. However, the postwar boom in higher education resulted in still higher quality students than in the 1930s, and substantially higher quality than in the 1920s. This result for the 1950s and 1960s is substantiated in Darley (1962), in which the records of college freshmen in specified colleges have been examined.

The data suggest a mean IQ of about the 40th percentile for those not entering college. There is a significant downward trend in $\bar{A}_{nc}$ over the period.[4] The value of $\bar{A}_c - \bar{A}_{nc}$, which describes how much more

[4] $\bar{A}_c$ and $\bar{A}_{nc}$ need not move in opposite directions because of differences in their weights.

TABLE 2 Fraction of high school graduates entering college at selected ability levels for various samples

Sample	Year	Percentile (A)			
		.25	.50	.75	.90
O'Brien	1925	.27	.36	.45	.51
		.36	.45	.54	.60
Benson	1929	.25	.36	.48	.54
		.34	.45	.57	.63
Barker	1934	.11	.23	.38	.46
		.26	.38	.53	.61
Phearman	1946	.12	.28	.46	.57
		.23	.39	.57	.68
Berdie*	1950	.24	.37	.54	.66
		.25	.38	.55	.67
Little*	1957	.14	.26	.44	.58
		.33	.45	.63	.76
Talent*	1960	.24	.41	.65	.83
		.31	.48	.72	.90
Berdie and Hood*	1961	.21	.37	.59	.74
		.34	.50	.72	.87

Note: The first line for each entry is the value calculated from the regression equation; the second line is this value adjusted to the United States population as a whole. A detailed discussion of the adjustment method appears in Appendix C.

*The nonlinear form of the regression equation was used for these samples; the linear form was used for the others. All equations are presented in the detailed discussion of the samples.

able the college students were, shows a very pronounced upward trend.

On the basis of these data it is apparent that the quality of college students has not declined. In fact, throughout this period of 40 years, during which a substantially greater percentage of high school graduates entered college, it has even noticeably increased. The basic explanation of this phenomenon is analyzed in the loss-of-talent discussion given below, but it can be summarized as follows. In the 1920s only about 60 percent of the most able high school graduates entered college, whereas by the 1960s the corresponding figure was about 90 percent.

To understand how $\bar{A}_c$ has shifted and to study the loss of talent in various time periods, we evaluate the equations presented below to determine the fraction of high school graduates entering college (E_{12}) at selected ability levels (A).[5] The selected values of A are .25, .50, .75,

---
[5] We have estimated both linear and nonlinear equations and have used the latter in our calculations when nonlinearities are significant. However, nearly identical results are obtained from the linear equations. Moreover, for the linear equations the results are almost the same whether education or ability is used as the dependent variable.

and .90. The last point should certainly include those people who are talented, while .75 lies well above the mean IQ percentile of college entrants. The value of .50 is the median of the distribution, though less than $\bar{A}_c$, while .25 is certainly indicative of the less able students. In Table 2 we present the results for various samples in both adjusted and unadjusted form, but in Figure 2 we present only the adjusted estimates.[6]

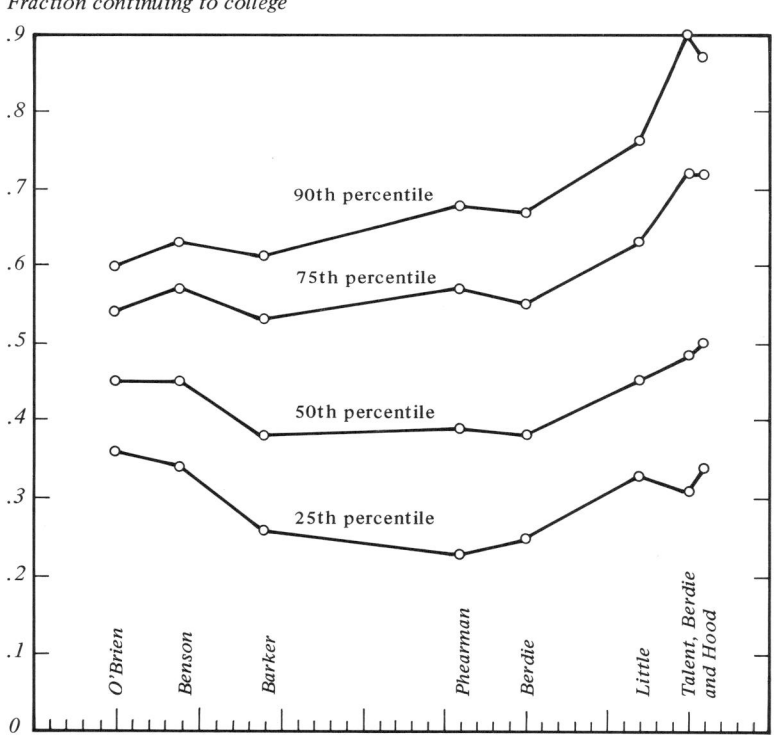

FIGURE 2 Fraction of high school graduates continuing to college at selected percentiles, adjusted

These results suggest the following general pattern. At the 90th and 75th percentiles, the percentage entering college has increased substantially over time. At the 50th percentile, the 1960 values are slightly

---

[6]This adjustment, as in the case of average ability levels, is intended to take into account differences in the percentage continuing in the sample and in the population.

FIGURE 3 Data points from O'Brien sample, 1925

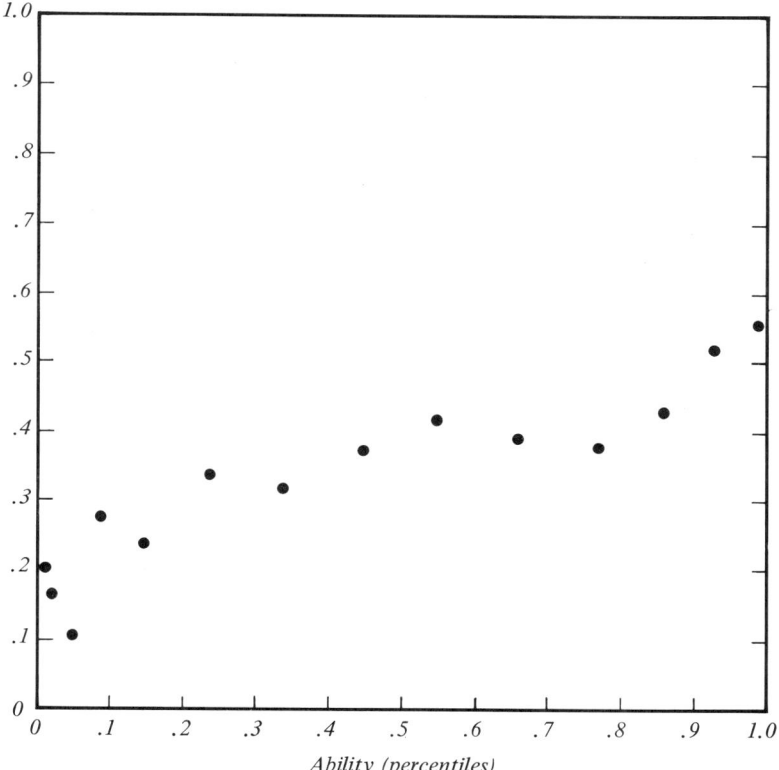

higher than those for the 1920s and the values for the 1930s and 1940s are substantially lower. At the 25th percentile, the fraction of high school graduates entering college appears to have fallen during the 1930s and 1940s, but by the 1960s is back to the 1920 level. We do not have exactly comparable data for the pre-World War I era, but the information on men in Yerkes (1921) indicates that the loss in talent (at the various percentiles) for high school graduates was about the same as in the late 1950s. Since less than 10 percent of the population graduated from high school, the loss of talent occurred at earlier educational levels.

As noted above, we estimated both linear and nonlinear equations. In explaining the loss of talent, we find no evidence that the coefficient on the nonlinear term (A^2) is significant in the samples for the period

FIGURE 4 Data points from Project Talent sample, 1960

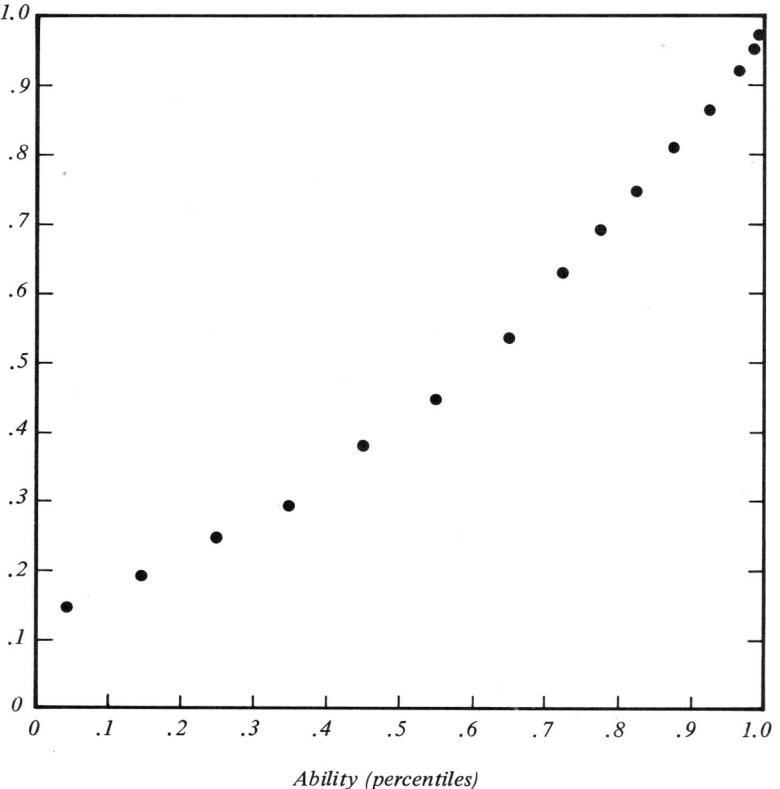

1920-1940. After the Second World War, however, the coefficient on this variable, which is always positive, is highly significant. To illustrate the difference between the prewar and postwar periods, we plot in Figures 3 and 4 (the O'Brien and Talent studies) the actual data points of two representative samples. The nonlinearity in the postwar sample is clearly evident.

Based on the percentage who enter college at various IQ levels, it is evident that in the 1950s and 1960s there was less loss of talent than in the 1920s and 1930s. It is interesting to speculate why less talent is lost now than earlier and why the average IQ level of college entrants has risen. To this end we have examined various histories of higher education in the United States, but except for certain comments in Jencks and Riesman (1968), none of these is very explicit on the subject.[7] We suggest that much of the shift occurred because of the changing financial constraints applicable to high school graduates over time. Before World War I very few people completed high school and very few parents could afford a college education, especially since depressions occurred frequently. In addition the available data indicate that (for males) college education differed sharply by ability level. The middle to late 1920s was a period of prosperity in which the high school population and the middle and upper classes grew rapidly. Partly because their income permitted it and partly for social reasons, there was a tendency for the children of these groups to attend college.[8] But since the correlation between bright students and wealthy parents was not that high, the distribution of college entrants by IQ was reasonably flat (a low selectivity coefficient). In addition, Jencks and Riesman (1968) argue that in the 1920s colleges as a whole were willing to take any person who applied.

The 1930s generated a whole new set of pressures as income fell, unemployment became rampant, and the high school population continued to expand faster than the population. In the post-World War II era, the percentages of students continuing to college in the upper IQ brackets rose sharply while those at the bottom rose only slightly. Some possible explanations for this development are that many more middle-class families could both afford to send their above-average children to school and wanted to send them because they believed schooling to be the road for advancement. In addition, the capital markets may have become more perfect with the advent of federal scholarships and loans. Finally, Jenks and Riesman suggest that, starting in the late 1940s, colleges that did not have enough facilities to accommodate the surging demand for space tried to select only the brightest students.[9]

Finally, separate results for males and females are available for some of the samples. The same general pattern over time holds for males and females separately and for the combined sample. The average ability levels of those continuing to college are approximately the same for males and females. As far as the loss of talent is concerned, the fraction

---

[7] However, the histories indicate that there was a growing trend over time in the amount of undergraduate training required by the traditional professional schools. In addition, many other occupations began to require a formal education as a prerequisite to entrance.

[8] See Goetsch (1940) for a discussion of college-going patterns by parental income.

[9] Jencks and Riesman (1968) argue that the colleges initially assumed the increase in demand to be a temporary phenomenon connected with the GI Bill.

of males continuing exceeds that of females at the selected percentiles discussed above, with the absolute differences becoming larger the higher the percentile.

For the period prior to the 1930s, we also estimated our equations—with data from Benson (1940) and Yerkes (1921)—for each grade after the sixth. There is a sharp drop in the slope coefficient after the completion of the eighth and twelfth grades. Although average ability increases with educational development, most of the gain occurs from the seventh through the twelfth grade.

Appendix A: Data and Results from the Various Studies Used in This Report

The above conclusions are, of course, based on a detailed examination of as many relevant samples as we could locate. To be relevant, a sample not only had to contain information on college attendance by IQ level, but the public record also had to contain enough data points to permit statistical investigation. In this appendix we will discuss in detail the various samples we have used and the results we obtained from each.

Since many of these studies were conducted before the Second World War and only a few of them were undertaken by economists, most contemporary economists will probably be unfamiliar with them. In addition, since these studies are conducted by different people at various times and places, there are differences in the populations sampled and in the designs of the samples. For these reasons we will have to describe each sample in some detail as we present our results.

As mentioned above, the ability measure (A) in each sample has been standardized by converting it into percentile standing based on the population of high school graduates. The education measure is the fraction of high school graduates, in any ability class, continuing to college.

Yerkes Study
The first group IQ tests were developed and used by the U.S. Army in the World War I. The Alpha version of this test was similar to tests now in use; the Beta version was designed for those who were illiterate. Robert M. Yerkes has presented much of the data on scores cross-classified by schooling, occupation, and other bases.[1] In most instances separate information is available for white native-born enlisted men, white foreign-born enlisted men, Negro enlisted men, and officers. There is evidence that the data on Negroes is affected by the cultural bias in the test. Since the same problem probably exists for the foreign

---

[1] The basic reference to the World War I tests is Yerkes (1921). All statements and references are from this volume unless otherwise noted. In our analysis we have used data from Tables 280, 281, and 393-395.

born, we have studied only the white native-born enlisted men and the officers. Further, we have excluded M.D.'s from the analysis since they have a lower IQ and higher educational attainment than other officers;[2] in addition, because of the nature of the army, M.D.'s are represented in the sample in a much larger proportion than in the population as a whole. We believe that this composition of the population corresponds closely to the makeup of our other samples from non-Southern states in the 1920's (except that females are excluded here).

A problem with these data is that the tests were given to people with different amounts of schooling. As noted earlier, although this method yields biased estimates, we can correct for it roughly. Another difficulty is that in order to relate schooling completed at the time of the test to IQ scores, we must assume either that all individuals had completed their schooling, or that (because of the war) everyone's recorded educational attainment was the same fraction of his final amount of schooling. These assumptions would be violated if students were allowed to volunteer for the army or if they were drafted from school. For World War I, however, Congress passed a law that specifically restricted volunteer army enlistments to one division.[3] But the enlisted men who were tested were all draftees.[4] Further, since the draft itself only applied to those 21-30 years of age, it is reasonable to assume that all precollege education was completed. Consequently, it is possible to use the sample of about 50,000 white, native-born enlisted men and 12,000 officers to study ability differences between males who enter college and males who only complete twelfth grade. It is also possible to study ability differences between these two groups and those with less than twelve years of schooling. Since the testees were between the ages of 21 and 30, they would have been born between 1887 and 1896; consequently, those who finished high school would have graduated approximately between 1905 and 1914.

Finally, when these data are grouped by occupation there is evidence that—because of draft exemptions—the people with higher IQ's in some occupations have been underrepresented.[5] Although this omission would be important if one were comparing average IQ levels by occupation, it will not affect our education-IQ estimates unless the functional relation for the excluded people differs from that of the included. There appears to be no good reason to assume such a difference exists.

---

[2] Compare Tables 280 and 393-395 in Yerkes (1921).

[3] See, for example, Miller (1968).

[4] The test results only apply to draftees and not pre-1917 recruits.

[5] For a discussion of revised estimates by occupation, see Bingham (1937) and Fryer (1922).

Appendix A: Data and results **27**

Yerkes published his data cross-classified by about 35 IQ groups and by (completed) years of schooling ranging from 0 through 12 years of college. It is possible, therefore, to determine the specific grades in which ability becomes crucial in determining future educational attainment. We will consider this particular question shortly, but first we present the results for the percentage of high school graduates who enter college:

(1) $\quad A = -.52 + 1.45 E_{12} \qquad \bar{R}^2 = .73$
$\qquad \;\; (4.1) \quad (8.4)$

In this and subsequent equations, the definitions of the variables are:

$\quad A \quad$ = the midpoint of the various IQ categories available. The categories are defined as ranges of percentiles such as 0 to 10th, or 25th to 40th percentile.

$\quad E_{12}$ = the fraction of high school graduates in a particular percentile range who entered college (or, in some instances, completed one year).

For each sample there are as many observations as there are IQ categories. Each number in parentheses is the ratio of the absolute value of the parameter to its standard error, while $\bar{R}^2$ is the coefficient of determination corrected for degrees of freedom. This regression, and all others given below that use grouped data, are estimated by weighting each sample point by the square root of the number of people in each ability class that contains the sample point.

The coefficient on E_{12} is about 1.5 and significant at the 1 percent level. Solving the equation for E_{12}, we find that as the percentile rank increases by one unit (e.g., 20th to 21st percentile), the percentage of high school graduates entering college rises by .70 percentage points.[6] The reciprocal of the coefficient of E will be denoted the "selectivity coefficient" in the discussions to follow.

Before considering the implications of this result two points must be acknowledged. As indicated in footnote 9 on page 14, the coefficient of 1.45 is biased upward and the bias is equal to the least squares estimate of λ in $z = \lambda E_{12} + v$. On the basis of the Learned and Wood data, we calculated λ to be about .15; therefore, our corrected estimate of the slope coefficient of E_{12} is 1.3, which has a reciprocal of .77. Thus, as a result, the selectivity after correction is even greater. As will become clear from our results for other samples and cohorts, even the selectivity coefficient of .7, which is biased downwards, is quite steep as compared with the decades immediately following.

While the estimate of the coefficient of E_{12} is biased upwards in (1), we showed earlier that the bias that would occur when A was the

---

[6]There is a poor fit at the very low and very high ability ranges. Consequently, the results should be used cautiously in these ranges.

independent variable could be positive or negative. Thus, it is not surprising that when we computed the comparable equation to (1), the coefficient on A was .37. In the follow-up samples presented below, where we would not expect a bias, the reciprocals of the coefficients on E are much closer to the coefficients on A.

We turn next to the results for different years of schooling. Since A refers to the percentile rank of high school graduates, it is inappropriate for scaling scores for other years of schooling. Hence, in the following equations our measure of ability is the recorded Alpha score. The results will not be directly comparable with other samples, but some intrasample conclusions can be drawn.

The method of analysis is as follows. Starting with the seventh grade we relate the mean score in each Alpha category to the percentage in each such category who continue to the next grade. For example, E_7 represents the number of people in a particular Alpha category who have an education greater than or equal to eight grades, divided by the number of people in that category who attended seven or more grades. Similarly, E_8 is equal to those in a given Alpha category with nine or more years of education divided by those with eight or more years. In general, $E_k = (\sum_{k+1}^{t} a_j) / (\sum_{k}^{t} a_j)$ where a_j is the number of people with j years of education in a given Alpha category, and t is the maximum number of years of schooling.

Since those in the age group 21-30 were subject to the draft and since college attendance did not confer a deferment, some college students may have had their recorded education terminated involuntarily; thus the equations using E_{13}, E_{14}, and E_{15} may be affected. However, this qualification presumably only applies to 21- and 22-year-olds and only to some of these; thus, our equations are probably not seriously in error. The results appear in Table 3.

Several points in the table are worthy of comment. The first point is that every estimate of b is significant at the 1 percent level. The second point concerns the pattern of the reciprocals of b, or the selectivity coefficients. Relatively little selection, or weeding-out, occurred at the end of the seventh or eleventh grades—that is, the 1/b values are .39 and .34. At the end of the eighth grade, which in many areas terminated pre-high school education, the greatest selectivity occurred—with a 1/b value of .68. Judging by the t values, this estimate of 1/b differs significantly from that for the seventh or eleventh grade. During grades nine and ten, selectivity is slightly more than for the seventh grade, but substantially less than at the entrance to high school. Upon graduation from high school, selectivity increases to a high level, second only to selectivity after the eighth grade. While the big college weeding-out process is at the stage of entering, selectivity during college remains at a substantial level. Thus the average of 1/b for grades thirteen, fourteen,

TABLE 3   World War I regressions by grades of education completed, and average IQ by grades completed

$$(\text{Alpha} = a + bE_k)$$

k	b	$\frac{1}{b}$	Average alpha score	Number of students in average
7	2.55 (18.7)	.39	53	7765
8	1.46 (26.4)	.68	69	14966
9	2.33 (17.4)	.43	89	4054
10	2.31 (15.9)	.43	96	3309
11	2.95 (13.0)	.34	105	2082
12	1.65 (7.9)	.61	119	3698
13	2.06 (10.2)	.49	117	1782
14	2.34 (16.8)	.43	126	2100
15	1.94 (14.8)	.52	134	2143

Note: $E_k = \sum_{k+1}^{t} a_j / \sum_{k}^{t} a_j$

where k is highest school grade completed. Data are for officers and native-born, white enlisted men. The sample size is about 50,000. Medical doctors are excluded.

and fifteen of about .47 is exceeded only by the 1/b values for the eighth and twelfth grades.

It should be recalled that the above equations will be biased because the Alpha scores are partly determined by years of schooling. But it is extremely unlikely that the bias varies enough from one year to the next to explain the differences in b for the eighth and twelfth grades, as compared with these values for grades on either side of eight and twelve.

Finally, the reader should realize that this analysis of selectivity is, in general, cumulative. That is, because attrition in each grade is related to mental ability, one would expect the average Alpha score of students who complete the eighth grade to exceed that of seventh grade students. Similarly, one would expect the scores of students who complete the ninth grade to be on the average better than those who finish the eighth grade, etc. The average Alpha scores for each grade (together with the numbers of students) can, in fact, be calculated directly from the Yerkes data and are presented in the right-hand columns of Table 3. The averages increase with grades completed, except for the thirteenth year. This means that the average ability level of those who drop out of college after one year is actually lower than the average of those who end their education after completing high school. Dropouts after two years, however, have a higher average ability than those who complete just high school. Further, although not reported here, the average ability of those with one and two years of graduate schooling is slightly below the ability level of those with four years of undergraduate schooling.

A comparable analysis cannot be carried out for World War II data. It is true that during World War II a substantial cross section of the population was in the military and was subjected to IQ testing in the form of the Army General Classification Test (A.G.C.T.). But unfortunately the data are not directly usable because the draft age was 18 and volunteers were encouraged. Indeed, the occupation of many of those who were tested was high school or college student.[7]

In addition to the data derived from the published records of the military, it is possible to obtain information on ability and education from follow-up studies. A number of these have been published in sufficient detail to permit analysis of the individual samples. We present now a discussion of these samples.

Proctor Study

As far as we have been able to determine, the earliest civilian (group) IQ test in which students were subsequently followed-up was conducted by William M. Proctor. In 1917-1918, Proctor tested about 1,600 students in San Francisco Bay Area high schools with the Army Alpha and Stanford Binet tests. His sample included male and female students enrolled in grades nine to twelve. Then, in a 1923 follow-up study, Proctor compiled the educational histories from 1917 through 1923 of a sample of 130 of the original 1,600 students.[8]

---

[7] See Stewart (1947).

[8] Since the students were drawn from the Stanford University area, the within-sample percentiles were not representative of the nation. Thus we used the following ability conversion procedure. We calculated the frequency distribution of high school students on the Stanford Binet from the information contained in the Benson study described below. Using this curve, we have converted the Proctor scores to a nationwide percentile basis.

The results for the 130 males and females combined are:

(2) $\quad A = -.39 + 1.00 E_{12} \quad \bar{R}^2 = .66$
$\quad\quad\quad (3.1)\ \ (5.6)$

where A is IQ percentile and E_{12} is percentage of high school graduates continuing their education. The slope coefficient, which is significant at the 1 percent level, implies a selectivity coefficient of 1.0. This is similar to the Yerkes estimate of .77, which of course is only for males.

For males we have:

(3) $\quad A = -.24 + .73 E_{12} \quad \bar{R}^2 = .27$
$\quad\quad\quad (1.1)\ (2.7)$

from which the selectivity coefficient is 1.4

For females the results are:

(4) $\quad A = -.20 + 1.18 E_{12} \quad \bar{R}^2 = .59$
$\quad\quad\quad (1.4)\ \ (5.1)$

The 1923 Proctor sample is quite useful, for it is the only one available for this time period and contains separate information for males and females. However, it should be recalled that only 130 students were tested and not all of these graduated from high school. In addition, all the students lived in Palo Alto and, although we used a special conversion method because we suspected this student body to be atypical, the equations may still reflect special circumstances. First, substantial evidence exists that students from urban and rural areas have different behavior. Moreover, college attendance in this period may have been crucially related to the nearness of a college. Finally, those students whose parents taught at Stanford probably had more psychological motivation to attend college. Thus, the above equations should be treated with caution, especially since the $\bar{R}^2$ for this sample is much lower than in most others.

Benson Study

The sample obtained by Viola Benson (1942), which has been extensively and ingeniously used by Becker (1964), is very unusual, since the IQ test (Haggerty Intelligence Examination) was given to approximately 2,000 students in the *sixth* grade in Minneapolis in 1923. In 1940 Miss Benson obtained information on the subsequent educational attainment of about 1,700 of these students.[9] In her thesis (Benson, 1940), the data are presented as the number of people in a given IQ range who achieved various levels of schooling from sixth grade through PhD.[10] This sample can be used to study the relationship between ability and education for pre-high school students, as well as high school entrants and high school graduates. Since the Benson data refer to students in

---

[9] One was still in college at the time of the study.

[10] In her article the data are condensed to five educational attainment groups.

the sixth grade, these students would have entered high school in about 1926, or nearly a decade after those in Proctor's and up to two decades after Yerkes' sample. No separate information on males and females is available.

The education for high school graduates is:
(5) $A = -.31 + 2.24E_{12}$ $\overline{R}^2 = .77$
       (1.6) (4.4)

The slope coefficient is significant at the 1 percent level. Solving the equation for E_{12}, we find that the selectivity coefficient is approximately .45. This selectivity coefficient is much lower than the estimate of .77 from Yerkes' data. Therefore, it appears that ability differences were more important in differentiating the percentage continuing to college in the early part of the century than in the 1920s.

Next we examine the data by years of schooling. Following the method used with Yerkes, we estimate equations for the fraction of students in each grade (by IQ class) who enter the next grade.[11] The equations are presented in Table 4. Since the IQ tests in Yerkes and Benson are scaled differently, it is not possible to compare the coefficients; however, the pattern of results can be compared.[12]

The greatest selectivity occurs at the end of the eighth grade (end of pre-high school education). During high school the selectivity coefficient falls from 1.2 to .2 in the eleventh grade. At the end of high school IQ becomes important in determining those who enter college, but selectivity is almost as strong during college as at the end of the twelfth grade. The Yerkes data, which refer to students educated two decades earlier, yielded strikingly similar results. There, as here, the eighth and twelfth grades were the crucial points in the selectivity process, with the selectivity coefficient being slightly larger for the eighth grade. In both samples selectivity was lowest in the eleventh grade and was also low in the seventh grade. College selectivity rates, after entrance, were substantial in both cases.

It is of some interest to examine the mean IQ of the students who terminated their education at various grades. These data are included in the right-hand columns of Table 4. Except for the eleventh and fourteenth grades (which are based on small samples) they show a continuous increase. They differ from the Yerkes data in that the average IQ of college dropouts is consistently above that of high school graduates not continuing their education.

---

[11] The Benson and Yerkes data differ slightly: in Benson, the students are classified by the last grade they entered; in Yerkes, the data are for the last grade completed.

[12] In addition, the Yerkes results are biased, but those from Benson are not. Moreover, Benson's data combine males and females.

TABLE 4 Benson regressions by grades of education completed, and average IQ by grades completed

$$(IQ = a + bE_k)$$

k	b	$\frac{1}{b}$	Average IQ	Number of students in average
7	1.84 (5.6)	.54	99.7	127
8	.85 (2.4)	1.17	101.5	202
9	1.48 (5.6)	.67	105.9	170
10	2.02 (2.0)	.50	114.0	118
11	4.10 (3.3)	.24	111.1	45
12	1.31 (4.2)	.96	116.6	581
13	1.39 (3.8)	.71	119.1	56
14	1.17 (2.8)	.81	118.9	27
15	.95 (1.1)	1.05	122.7	11

O'Brien Study

In the early 1920s the Terman Group Test of Mental Ability was administered to more than 4,000 juniors and seniors from approximately 160 Kansas high schools. These students were followed through high school graduation, and college records of those who attended college were obtained by F. P. O'Brien (1928). Unfortunately, data are not available for girls and boys separately. The basic results for students tested in their senior year, after conversion to our standard form, are:

(6) $\quad A = -.48 + 2.72 E_{12} \quad \bar{R}^2 = .86$
$\quad\quad\quad (3.3) \quad (7.2)$

This equation is similar to that of the Benson study, suggesting a stable relationship between A and E for high school graduates of the 1920s.

Barker Study

Richard W. Barker (1937) studied 3,767 students who graduated from 148 Iowa high schools in 1934. In the fall of 1935, a questionnaire was sent to the high schools of these students to determine if they were attending college. The ability measure used was a composite measure based on all the "Iowa Every-Pupil Tests" the graduate had taken during his four years in high school. (In general 13 tests were given each year.) This composite measure was transmitted into percentile scores with the total sample as base. Data for seven ability classes are available for males and females separately. The results for the combined sample, and then for males and females separately, are:

(8) $\quad A = .05 + 1.87 E_{12} \quad \bar{R}^2 = .83$
$\quad\quad\quad (.04) \quad (4.5)$

(9) $\quad A = -.06 + 2.03 E_{12} \quad \bar{R}^2 = .80$
$\quad\quad\quad (.5) \quad (4.6)$

(10) $\quad A = .14 + 1.63 E_{12} \quad \bar{R}^2 = .75$
$\quad\quad\quad (1.4) \quad (4.3)$

Wolfle and Smith Study

In the mid 1950s, as part of a study for the Commission on Human Resources and Advanced Training, Dael Wolfle and Joseph Smith collected data on income in 1953, rank in high school class, IQ, post-high school education, and many other sociodemographic factors for some high school graduates of the 1930s. The basic data for men in summary form were published in Wolfle and Smith (1956).[13] While the original data in this study are no longer extant, Dr. Wolfle has kept extensive cross-tabulations of the information and has generously supplied us with these tabulations. Our analysis will be based on these printouts; our discussion of the data will be based on Wolfle and Smith (1956).

The samples of male and female students were drawn from Minnesota, Illinois, and Rochester, New York. We analyzed the Minnesota sample but not the other two, since they contained too few ability classes.

The Minnesota population covered every high school in Minnesota and included all graduates of 1938 who ranked in the upper 60% of their classes or who scored in the upper half of the distribution of all high school students on the American Council of Education Psychological Exam (ACE). A randomly selected sample of 10% of all 1938 Minnesota graduates was also surveyed. (ibid., p. 209).

The response rate (returned as a fraction of delivered questionnaires) for the Minnesota sample was .68. Unfortunately for our purposes here, there was a tendency for high school graduates who continued their education to respond more than proportionately as compared with those who did not continue. Consequently, in a regression of ability on

---

[13] These data are discussed in Anderson (1950), Anderson and Berning (1941), Becker (1964), Denison (1964), and Wolfle (1960).

education both the slope coefficient and the intercept will be biased downward.

Male high school graduates of 1938 were subject to the draft in World War II and were able to claim GI education benefits after the war. Since the literature of the 1920s and 1930s indicates that financial constraints were very important in determining the demand for college education, the GI Bill could have had substantial effects on the choice between work and college.[14] Indeed, the actual educational attainment in 1939, as presented in Anderson and Berning's initial follow-up survey, indicates that only half as many people entered college then as when Wolfle and Smith compiled their data. This result can, of course, be partially attributed to the response effect noted above.

For Minnesota we have information on the percentage of high school seniors who entered college by decile rank on the ACE exam.[15] The estimated equation is:

(11) $A = -1.10 + 2.36E_{12}$ $\bar{R}^2 = .89$
         (7.3) (10.2)

In this equation, E_{12} is significant at the 1 percent level implying a selectivity coefficient of .42, which is very close to those estimated from the O'Brien and Benson data.

Although this equation is estimated from data that included males and females, it is possible to obtain separate information for each of the sexes. The relevant equations for males and females respectively are:

(12) $A = -1.42 + 2.50E_{12}$ $\bar{R}^2 = .83$
         (5.3) (7.1)
(13) $A = -.97 + 2.41E_{12}$ $\bar{R}^2 = .79$
         (5.6) (8.1)

All the equations are similar, although the intercepts differ somewhat because fewer females attend college. The equations for males can be compared with those estimated from the Yerkes and Proctor data. It appears that in the Wolfle and Smith Minnesota data the selectivity coefficient is approximately one-half to one-third as large as for these earlier studies.

Phearman Study

In 1946-1947, L. T. Phearman (1948) compared Iowa high school graduates who entered college with those who did not. His sample consisted of 2,616 high school seniors from 192 Iowa schools that were selected as representative of the various sizes of schools in the state. The ability measure used was the percentile rank on the "Iowa Tests of Educa-

---

[14] See, for example, Goetsch (1940).

[15] Following the usual census procedure, we have excluded vocational training from college education.

tional Development" that the students took in the fall of 1946. Attendance or nonattendance at college was verified in the fall of 1947 by follow-up letters to both the students and high school principals. The results for the combined sample, and separately for males and then females, are:

(18) $\quad A = .09 + 1.42 E_{12} \quad\quad \bar{R}^2 = .78$
$\quad\quad\quad (1.3)\ \ (7.3)$
(19) $\quad A = .14 + 1.26 E_{12} \quad\quad \bar{R}^2 = .75$
$\quad\quad\quad (2.1)\ \ (6.8)$
(20) $\quad A = .04 + 1.55 E_{12} \quad\quad \bar{R}^2 = .77$
$\quad\quad\quad (.6)\ \ (7.2)$

The coefficients are considerably lower than those of the earlier studies, suggesting the possibility of a significant change in the selectivity coefficient from the prewar to the postwar period. Several studies undertaken in the 1950s, analyzed in detail below, support this view and indicate that more change occurred in the 1950s.

Berdie Studies

In 1950, R. Berdie (1954) studied the post-high school *plans* of over 90 percent of Minnesota's high school seniors in public and private schools. Test scores on the ACE (1947 form) college aptitude test and rank in class were available for all students. A follow-up study one year after these students graduated revealed the extent to which their plans were fulfilled. Berdie reports, "although many students changed their plans, the overall proportions of students actually pursuing the various plans were close to the proportions of those who had chosen these plans the year before" (ibid., p. 64). Of the students who said they were planning on attending college, 84 percent actually entered. A further follow-up study of this group in 1954 by Corcoran and Keller (1957) provided additional information. In particular, it contained a comparison of college plans and actual college attendance by ability levels. Their tables indicate that for each of the IQ classes the fraction of students planning to attend college is nearly identical with the fraction actually attending. In view of this result, we have used the percentage planning to continue at each ability level from the original 1950 study as an estimate of those actually continuing.[16]

In 1961, Berdie and A. Hood (1963) conducted another study similar to that of 1950. For most students the Minnesota Scholastic Aptitude test score was available—having been administered during the winter of the junior year in high school. Students' post-high school plans were

---

[16] The original study is used because it provides twice as many IQ classes as the Corcoran and Keller study.

elicited through use of a questionnaire completed in the senior year by 97 percent of all graduating seniors in Minnesota.

In the spring of 1962 a follow-up letter sent to a random sample of students revealed that approximately 92 percent of those who planned to attend college actually were doing so one year later. In view of this result, we have used the data on college plans by ability level to reflect actual attendance.

We consider first the results for students who graduated from high school in 1950. Our equation for male and female graduates combined is:[17]

(21) $\quad A = -.14 + 1.61 E_{12} \quad \bar{R}^2 = .98$
$\quad\quad\quad (3.7)\ (18.6)$

E_{12} is significant at the 1 percent level, yielding a selectivity coefficient of .62.[18] This estimate is substantially different from those of the O'Brien, Benson, and Wolfle and Smith Minnesota studies, but not from the Barker and Phearman studies. The separate equations for males and females respectively are:

(22) $\quad A = -.15 + 1.49 E_{12} \quad \bar{R}^2 = .98$
$\quad\quad\quad (4.2)\ (20.1)$

(23) $\quad A = -.14 + 1.76 E_{12} \quad \bar{R}^2 = .98$
$\quad\quad\quad (3.3)\ (16.2)$

The Berdie and Hood data on college plans in 1961, which we treat as comparable with our other information, yield for males and females combined:[19]

(24) $\quad A = -.03 + 1.29 E_{12} \quad \bar{R}^2 = .98$
$\quad\quad\quad (.89)\ (20.8)$

E_{12} is significant at the 1 percent level, and the selectivity coefficient is higher than the one estimated from the earlier Berdie study. The separate equations for males and females respectively are:

(25) $\quad A = -.05 + 1.23 E_{12} \quad \bar{R}^2 = .98$
$\quad\quad\quad (1.7)\ (21.7)$

(26) $\quad A = -.00 + 1.37 E_{12} \quad \bar{R}^2 = .98$
$\quad\quad\quad (.05)\ (19.8)$

---

[17] The nonlinear form of this equation with E_{12} as the dependent variable, which was used in the "loss of talent" discussion above (Figure 2), is:
$\quad E_{12} = .16 + .21 A + .38 A^2 \quad \bar{R}^2 = .99$
$\quad\ (8.8)\ (2.4)\ \ (4.6)$

[18] The results using the Corcoran and Keller follow-up are almost identical—the coefficient of E_{12} is 1.66.

[19] The nonlinear form is:
$\quad E_{12} = .09 + .36 A + .40 A^2 \quad \bar{R}^2 = .99$
$\quad\ (12.7)(10.5)\ \ (12.0)$

This pattern of results is the same as for the 1950 study in that the slope coefficient is higher for females than males, with the combined result in between.

Assuming for the moment that Minnesota is typical of the 1950-1960 era, we can draw the following conclusions. First, selectivity coefficients are greater in this era than in the 1920s or 1930s. Second, it appears that between 1950 and 1961 the coefficient increased by a statistically significant amount.

The extent to which Minnesota is typical of the nation can be gauged on the basis of results for other states, or for the country as a whole. The results we will present shortly strongly resemble the Minnesota equations. It is also useful to note that the Benson study was drawn from Minneapolis, and the Wolfle and Smith data were from Minnesota. While the relevant factors that affect the ability-education relation in one state vis-a-vis another state could change over time, a comparison of the various Minnesota studies is probably meaningful.

Little Study

J. Kenneth Little (1958) has analyzed the students at Wisconsin high schools who were seniors during the academic year 1956-1957. In the spring of 1957 approximately 95 percent of Wisconsin's high school seniors filled out questionnaires that included information on their plans beyond high school. The class rank and percentile scores on the Henmon-Nelson Tests of Mental Ability were obtained for most graduates. In the fall of 1957 a questionnaire was sent to the parents of approximately one-sixth of the graduates from each school. This sample indicated that 90 percent of the seniors who planned to attend college were actually enrolled. We have used these data on educational plans to obtain the following results for the IQ deciles for males and females combined:[20]

(29) $\quad A = .04 + 1.55 E_{12} \qquad \bar{R}^2 = .95$
$\qquad (.9) \ (13.1)$

The coefficient of E_{12} lies between the Berdie estimates for 1950 and 1961, as we would have expected. The results, respectively, for males and females are:

(30) $\quad A = .02 + 1.44 E_{12} \qquad \bar{R}^2 = .96$
$\qquad (.6) \ (15.3)$

(31) $\quad A = .05 + 1.74 E_{12} \qquad \bar{R}^2 = .94$
$\qquad (1.1) \ (12.3)$

---

[20] The nonlinear form is:
$\qquad E_{12} = .06 + .19 A + .42 A^2 \qquad \bar{R}^2 = .98$
$\qquad (2.3) \ (1.6) \quad (3.6)$

This pattern of results agrees with those of the Phearman and the Berdie studies in that the slope coefficient is smallest for males and largest for females.

Project Talent Study

In 1959 a massive attempt to collect and analyze nationwide educational and mental ability data on students was begun. A great deal of socioeconomic and mental ability data on students in different grades has been collected by Project Talent (1964). Of particular interest to us are those students who graduated from high school in 1960. Approximately 88,000 were sent questionnaires one year later in an attempt to determine, among other things, whether they were or had been in college. About 70 percent of the students responded. To eliminate nonresponse bias, a random sample of 5 percent of those who did not reply were located by other means, and this group was used to represent the nonresponders.

The results for the combined sample, and then for males and females separately, are:[21]

(33) $\quad A = -.03 + 1.17 E_{12} \qquad \bar{R}^2 = .95$
$\qquad (1.1)\ (20.0)$

(34) $\quad A = -.11 + 1.18 E_{12} \qquad \bar{R}^2 = .99$
$\qquad (7.2)\ (44.9)$

(35) $\quad A = -.02 + 1.17 E_{12} \qquad \bar{R}^2 = .90$
$\qquad (.6)\ (14.4)$

These results are very similar to those of the 1961 Berdie study.

---

[21] The nonlinear form is:
$\quad E_{12} = .14 + .26 A + .57 A^2 \qquad \bar{R}^2 = .99$
$\quad\ \ (20.9)\ (8.3)\quad (19.4)$

Appendix B: Other Studies

Mention should be made at this point of three other studies in which ability measures and educational attainment are available—those of Thorndike and Hagen (1959), Terman and Oden (1947), and Learned and Wood (1938).

The Thorndike and Hagen data are drawn from a group of males who were tested by the Air Force as part of a search for bombardiers, pilots, and navigators in World War II. Although the tests were conducted throughout the war, this sample was drawn from those who took a single form of the test used from June to December 1943. Before taking this test, the individuals first had to pass an Army General Classification Test (AGCT) with a score equivalent to a college sophomore. We have not analyzed these data here since the sample is not representative of the high school graduate population in general.

In 1920, Lewis M. Terman began a study of 1,000 elementary and high school students (in nonrural California) whose IQ placed them in the top 2 percent of intelligence (i.e., their scores were 140 and over in the Stanford-Binet Scale). These students were periodically resurveyed until the end of the 1950s. However, the Terman data involve such a special IQ range that we have not analyzed them in this paper.

The Learned and Wood sample discussed above consists of about 70 percent of Pennsylvania's high school seniors in 1928 (28,000 students). The published data include information on the IQ distribution of the seniors who went to college, to vocational schools, or into various occupations. Separate information is published for males and females in the form of charts, with the 10th, 25th, 50th, 75th, and 90th percentile scores indicated for the various breakdowns. We attempted to convert this to the percentage of people in various IQ classes who entered college.[1] Unfortunately, the regression results were

---

[1] For each percentile listed above, we take the raw Otis score for the sample as a whole. From the frequency distribution of those entering college, we determine the number of students with raw scores less than the 10th percentile score, greater than the 10th but less than the 25th, etc.

very sensitive to the arbitrary interpolation procedure required to put the data into desired form; consequently we have not included this sample in our analysis. We have, however, used the information from this study to estimate the extent to which schooling affects IQ, as discussed in the analysis of Yerkes' data.

In addition to the data sources described above, we obtained a number of studies that provide some relevant information for our purposes, such as the percent of seniors going on to college by IQ quartile. However, since these studies do not provide enough data points to permit each sample to be analyzed separately, they have been combined with others from corresponding time periods in estimating the selectivity coefficients for the period 1945-1957, and for the 1960s.[2] A brief description of these studies follows.

1 A sample of 1566 Arkansas high school graduates of 1949 reported by Charles G. Morehead (1950). The actual data points, which were combined with others from the 1945-1957 period, are:

A	E_{12}
95.0	57
82.5	52
12.5	14

where A is measured in percentiles and E_{12} is in percent.

2 A sample of 1,170 high school graduates of 1960 reported by Charles B. Nam (1962). The data points, which were combined with those of the 1961 Berdie and Hood study and the Project Talent study, are:

E	E_{12}
87.5	67.2
62.5	38.2
37.5	24.8
12.5	15.5

---

[2]Additional pieces of information are available in Bridgman (1960). A comparison of our regression equations with these data suggests that they are consistent.

Appendix C: Adjustment Procedure for Average-Ability and Loss-of-Talent Calculations

As mentioned in the text, the estimates in Figures 1 and 2 have been adjusted to national levels. Such an adjustment is necessary when comparing results from a number of different samples in which the fraction of high school students continuing to college differs from the population value. We have calculated this fraction for each sample, and for the United States as a whole, for the year in which each sample was taken. Suppose that for a particular sample we denote the sample fraction continuing as E_{12}^S, and the corresponding population fraction as E_{12}^P. Consider first the adjustments needed in our loss of talent estimates. These consist of adding $E_{12}^P - E_{12}^S$ to the regression-calculated estimate of the fraction continuing at each of the selected percentiles. It is necessary to make the same correction at each ability level since no nationwide data are available on the fraction continuing by ability. The following interpretation of our adjustment method may be enlightening. If our estimated sample relationship is written as $E_{12} = e + fA$, then we are assuming that the population relationship is $E_{12} = (E_{12}^P - E_{12}^S + e) + fA$. Since our sample relation is constrained to hold at the sample means, that is, $\overline{E}_{12}^S = e + f\overline{A}^S$, and since $\overline{A}$ is the same in the sample as in the population, this adjustment allows the population relationship to pass through the means.

An alternative adjustment procedure is to multiply the sample values of E_{12} at each percentile by E_{12}^P/E_{12}^S. The choice between the ratio and the absolute adjustment factor depends on one's assumption about the reason for the discrepancy between the sample and population means. The following line of reasoning suggests that the absolute adjustment is more appropriate than the proportional one. For the Little and Talent studies, which are separated by only three years, one would expect the population relationships to be fairly similar. The coefficients on education in the sample relationship $A = h + kE_{12}$ are 1.55 and 1.17, respectively, for these samples. If the ratio adjustments are applied to convert them to population relations, then the divergence between these slope coefficients becomes much greater, since the Little sample requires a significantly larger adjustment than the other.[1] This does not seem to be a reasonable result. On the other hand, the absolute adjustment method leaves the slope coefficients unchanged.

Adjustment must also be made in $\bar{A}_c$ and $\bar{A}_{nc}$. Since we are assuming that the fraction continuing at each ability level is $E_{12}^P - E_{12}^S$ above the sample value, then the population average ability level of those continuing will be given by $(.5 E_{12}^P - E_{12}^S) + \bar{A}_c E_{12}^S)/E_{12}^P$ and the population average ability level of those not continuing will be $\bar{A}_{nc}(1 - E_{12}^S) - .5(E_{12}^P - E_{12}^S)/(1 - E_{12}^P)$.

Most of our estimates of the fraction of high school graduates continuing to college are obtained from *The Statistical Abstract of the United States* for 1970. Unfortunately, data are not presented there for the 1920s or for 1946. For these years we have based our estimates on census data. For the O'Brien and Benson samples of 1925 and 1929, we have obtained from the 1950 census the fraction of high school graduates in the 35-44 age group who attended college (41 percent). These persons would have been 18 (and hence high school graduates) in the years 1924-1933. Since census coverage may differ from that in the *Abstract*, we have also obtained from the 1950 census the fraction continuing for the periods 1934-1938 (34 percent). The absolute difference between this value and the value for 1934-1938 from the *Abstract* (38 percent) was used to adjust the correction factor for the 1920s. We have followed exactly the same procedure for 1946.

---

[1] In fact, the implied slope coefficient would be equal to those in the 1920s.

References

Abramovitz, M.: A Review Article of E. F. Denison, "The Sources of Economic Growth in the United States," *American Economic Review*, vol. 52, no. 4, September 1962.

Anderson, G. Lester: "What Happens to Minnesota's High School Graduates?," in *Higher Education in Minnesota*, Minnesota Commission on Higher Education, University of Minnesota Press, Minneapolis, 1950.

Anderson, G. Lester, and T. J. Berning: "What Happens to Minnesota High School Graduates?," *Studies in Higher Education*, University of Minnesota Committee on Educational Research, Biennial Report, 1938-1940, University of Minnesota Press, Minneapolis, 1941.

Astin, Alexander W.: "Undergraduate Achievement and Institutional Excellence," *Science*, vol. 161, pp. 661-667, August 1968.

Barker, Richard W.: "The Educational and Vocational Careers of High School Graduates Immediately Following Graduation in Relation to Their Scholastic Abilities," master's thesis, State University of Iowa, 1937.

Becker, Gary S.: *Human Capital*, National Bureau of Economic Research, New York, 1964.

Benson, Viola E.: "The Intelligence and Later Scholastic Success of Sixth Grade Pupils," master's thesis, University of Minnesota, 1940.

Benson, Viola E.: "The Intelligence and Later Scholastic Success of Sixth Grade Pupils," *School and Society*, vol. 55, pp. 163-167, Fall 1942.

Berdie, Ralph F.: *After High School–What?*, University of Minnesota, Minneapolis, 1954.

Berdie, Ralph, et al.: *Who Goes to College? Comparison of Minnesota College Freshmen, 1930-1960*, University of Minnesota, Minneapolis, 1962.

Berdie, Ralph, and Albert B. Hood: *Trends in Post-High School Plans Over an 11-Year Period*, Cooperative Research Project No. 951, Student Counseling Bureau, University of Minnesota, Minneapolis, 1963.

Bingham, Walter V.: *Aptitudes and Aptitude Testing*, Harper and Row, New York, 1937.

Bridgman, Donald S.: "Where the Loss of Talent Occurs and Why," in *The Search for Talent, College Admissions (7)*, College Entrance Examination Board, New York, 1960.

Brubacher, John S., and Willis Rudy: *Higher Education in Transition*, Harper and Row, New York, 1958.

Corcoran, Mary, and Robert J. Keller: "College Attendance of Minnesota High School Seniors," *A Report Prepared for the Governor's Committee on Higher Education*, Minneapolis, January 1957.

Darley, John C.: *Promise and Performance: A Study of Ability and Achievement in Higher Education*, Center for the Study of Higher Education, University of California, Berkeley, 1962.

Denison, Edward F.: "Measuring the Contribution of Education (and the Residual) to Economic Growth," in *The Residual Factor and Economic Growth*, OECD, Paris, 1964.

Denison, Edward F.: *The Sources of Economic Growth in the United States*, Committee for Economic Development, New York, 1961.

DeVane, Clyde W.: *Higher Education in Twentieth-Century America*, Cambridge, Mass., 1965.

Finch, Frank H.: "Enrollment Increases and Changes in the Mental Level of the High School Population," *Applied Psychology Monograph*, no. 10, 1946.

Folger, John K., and Charles B. Nam: *Education of the American Population* (A 1960 Census Monograph), U.S. Department of Commerce, Washington, D.C., 1967.

Fryer, Douglas: "Occupational Intelligence Standards," *School and Society*, vol. 16, pp. 273-277, 1922.

Goetsch, Helen B.: *Parental Income and College Opportunities*, Columbia University, New York, 1940.

Jencks, Christopher, and David Riesman: *The Academic Revolution*, Doubleday and Company, Garden City, N.Y., 1968.

Learned, William S., and Ben D. Wood: *The Student and His Knowledge*, The Carnegie Foundation for the Advancement of Teaching, Bulletin No. 29, New York, 1938.

Little, James K.: *A State-Wide Inquiry into Decisions of Youth about Education beyond High School*, University of Wisconsin, Madison, 1958.

Miller, James C.: *Why the Draft? The Case for a Volunteer Army*, Penguin, Baltimore, 1968.

Morehead, Charles: "What's Happening to Our High School Seniors?," *Journal of Arkansas Education*, vol. 23, April 1950.

Nam, Charles B., and James D. Cowhig: "Factors Related to College Attendance of Farm and Nonfarm High School Graduates: 1960," *Farm Population*, Department of Commerce and Department of Agriculture, Economic Research Service, Census-ERS, series P-27, no. 32, Washington, D.C., 1962.

O'Brien, F. P.: "Mental Ability with Reference to Selection and Retention of College Students," *Journal of Educational Research*, vol. 18, no. 2, pp. 136-143, September 1928.

Phearman, L. T.: "Comparisons of High School Graduates Who Go to College with Those Who Do Not Go to College," dissertation, Education Department of the Graduate College of the State University of Iowa, Iowa City, June 1948.

Proctor, William M.: "Educational Research and Statistics," *School and Society*, vol. 42, no. 1093, December 1935.

Proctor, William M.: "The Use of Psychological Tests in the Educational and Vocational Guidance of High School Pupils," *Journal of Educational Research Monographs*, no. 1, Public School Publishing Company, Bloomington, Ill., October 1923.

Project Talent: *The American High-School Student*, Cooperative Research Project No. 635, University of Pittsburgh, 1964.

Stewart, Naomi: "A.G.C.T. Scores of Army Personnel Grouped by Occupation," *Occupations*, vol. 26, 1947.

Taubman, Paul, and Terence Wales: "Education as an Investment and a Screening Device," National Bureau of Economic Research, (Mimeographed.) New York, 1972.

Terman, Lewis M., and Melita H. Oden: *Genetic Studies of Genius, Volume IV, The Gifted Child Grows Up*, Stanford University Press, Stanford, 1947.

Thorndike, Robert L., and E. Hagen: *Ten Thousand Careers*, John Wiley and Sons, New York, 1959.

Wolfle, Dael: *America's Resources of Specialized Talent*, The Report of the Commission on Human Resources and Advanced Training, Harper Brothers, New York, 1954.

Wolfle, Dael: "Economics and Educational Values," *The Review of Economics and Statistics*, vol. 42, August 1960 (Supplement).

Wolfle, Dael, and Joseph G. Smith: "The Occupational Value of Education for Superior High-School Graduates," *Journal of Higher Education*, vol. 27, pp. 201-213, 1956.

Yerkes, R. M. (ed.): "Psychological Examining in the U.S. Army," *Memoirs of the National Academy of Sciences*, G.P.O., Washington, D.C., 1921.

/378.73T222M>C1/